100 THAI WORDS THAT MAKE
YOU SOUND
THAI

SECOND EDITION

Copyright © Stephen Saad, 2016

Second edition published by Arun Press, 2016.

The right of Stephen Saad to be identified as the Author of the Work has been asserted by him in accordance with the Copyright,
Designs and Patents Act 1988.

All rights reserved.

This book is sold subject to the condition it shall not, by way of trade or otherwise, be circulated in any form or by any means, electronic or otherwise without the publisher's prior consent.

ISBN 978-1-911079-14-9

FOREWORD

As a professional language teacher (English, French, German & Russian), I am well aware of the challenges faced by learners when tackling a new language. When I moved to Thailand almost 18 years ago, I faced different challenges in trying to master the Thai language: a complicated writing system employing 76 consonants and vowels, rather than the 26 or so I was used to in European languages, and a tone system where getting the right tone is vital for effective communication.

Travelling 2 or 3 times a month on business to different countries in S.E. Asia has meant that I never had the time to master reading and writing in Thai, although I have rudimentary reading skills and can converse reasonably well on a day-to-day basis, exchange pleasantries on the weather and the traffic with taxi drivers, order food and question my daughters (in Thai & English) on what they did in school. But I understand little of what is being said on the news bulletins on Thai television and would not be able to hold a conversation on the latest developments in Thai politics.

So I guess I am like thousands of "farangs" living in Thailand: I can get by, but would like to be able to expand my vocabulary and be a more effective speaker when conversing with Thais on a daily basis. These 100 Thai words are the ideal way for me to achieve that. It will mean some extra work absorbing and practising all of the extremely useful words and phrases in this book, but I am prepared to put in the effort, because I can see from my own language training and experience that Steve Saad has put together just the right collection to bring my spoken Thai up to a higher level.

David Wilson

BA (Hons) Modern Languages, MLitt (Oxford) FRSA
Nakhon Ratchasima, November 2015

As a Thai language teacher, I'm happy to see something a little different coming out to the market. I've been in the Thai teaching industry for almost a decade and have always felt that textbooks for intermediate learners are lacking. Thai materials on the market, most of which are intended for beginners, often teach similar content. This makes it hard for someone who has already passed the beginner level to move on to a more advanced one. This book is one of those rare materials that focuses on teaching something new to learners of a higher level. You won't have to go through all those grammar rules that you already know again. Last but not least, the book is not just going to provide you with new knowledge but also interesting insights into the Thai language as well as the culture from a perspective of an author who has spent years living in Thailand.

Yuki Tachaya

Professional teacher of Thai as a foreign language and developer of Thai teaching materials "PickupThai Podcast"

www.pickup-thai.com

yuki.tachaya@pickup-thai.com

ACKNOWLEDGEMENTS

I would like to thank the following people for their help and support, without whom completing this book would not be possible:

Bangorn Maneekong – for all her help and advice with writing the Thai script and for being my wife!

Anonglak Songprakone – for editing the book and for her support and encouragement from the very start to make this a reality.

Yuki Tachaya – for editing parts of the book and providing insight into some of the more subtle aspects of Thai

Ali Dewji – for not only publishing the book but all his advice and suggestions on the design and marketing

Catherine Wentworth – for reviewing the draft, her advice and insight.

David Wilson – for reviewing the draft and confirming that this book is indeed very helpful for his Thai.

James Higbie – for all his advice on the book itself as well as all the process involved in publishing a book.

Mike Critchley – for his advice on publishing and language books in general.

Callan Anderson – for his help with understanding e-books and general publishing matters.

CONTENTS

Preface	8
About the author	16
Introduction	23
Transliteration method and guide to pronunciation	32
100 Thai words that make you sound Thai	36
1. **arai yang nee(-a)** *something like that / etc*	38
2. **dtang tae...** *since...*	40
3. **teung mae waa...** *even though...*	42
4. **meuan gun** *the same as each other / also / agree*	44
5. **ta yang nan / ngun** *in that case*	45
6. **gaw** *no literal meaning / also*	46
7. **krup** *no literal meaning*	48
8. **nai kana tee** *whereas / at the same time / while / all the while*	50
9. **riap rooi** *prim and proper / well mannered / finished / complete*	52
10. **laeo gun** *in that case / I'll settle for / no specific meaning*	54
11. **jing jing (laeo)** *Actually*	56
12. **ja bawk hai** *I can tell you (that for sure) / I'm telling you*	57
13. **seung** *which*	58
14. **yang dee** *still good / ok*	60
15. **leua wai** *left over / leave it there for...*	62
16. **kawn*-kaang** *pretty much / quite a bit*	64
17. **bpo-ka-dti** *normally*	66
18. **nee-ngai** *here it is*	67
19. **krai ja bpai roo** *who would know / how am I supposed to know*	68
20. **yok dtua yaang** *I'll give you an example / for example*	70
21. **dang nan / praw cha...** *therefore*	72
22. **suan...** *on his / her part / as for him / her*	73
23. **baang tee** *perhaps / maybe / sometimes*	74
24. **nai kwaam bpen jing** *in reality*	76
25. **taa mai kit arai maak** *if you are not that fussy / if you don't mind*	77
26. **laeo gaw** *and then*	78
27. **gaw daai** *ok / sure / no problem / whatever / maybe*	79
28. **saa-maad...daai** *able to / can*	80
29. **som-mood (waa)** *assume / let's say / suppose*	82
30. **ao bpen waa** *how about this...? / let's settle for...*	84
31. **taeb** *almost*	85
32. **gaw leuy** *and so / therefore*	86
33. **dtok-long..** *so / in the end*	88
34. **dtaai laeo** *Oh my god!*	90
35. **koi koi** *gradually / little by little*	92
36. **dtaw bpai** *in the future / next*	93
37. **kon la reuang...** *a whole different story / person / point*	95
38. **reu bplao** *or not*	96
39. **laeo yang ngai?...** *and then? / so?*	97
40. **keu... / (gaw) keu waa** *it is / it's like this...*	98
41. **ka-naad nan (gaw...)** *in spite of that / even if we take that into account*	99
42. **chai mai la?** *right?! / am I right or what?*	100
43. **mai koi daai..** *can't really...*	102
44. **meuan gup waa** *it's like / seems like / it's almost as if*	104
45. **ja daai...** *so that... / in order to*	105
46. **chohk dee** *good luck*	106
47. **sa-mai nan / nee** *in those days / these days*	107

48. **taen tee** *instead of*	108
49. **jon / jon gwaa...** *until / until after*	109
50. **poot teung (waa)** *talking about that... / now that you mention that*	110
51. **suk wan (neung)** *one day*	111
52. **wan dtaw maa** *the next day*	112
53. **krai gaw mai** *roo don't know who that is / don't recognize that person*	113
54. **yoo tee...** *is / it's to do with...*	114
55. **keun yoo gup waa** *it depends on / it's to do with*	115
56. **aang waa / aang teung** *mention / claim / refer to*	116
57. **laew ja tam tam-mai?** *and why would you do that? / what's the use / point?*	117
58. **yang raeng** *a lot*	118
59. **meua rai ja set...** *when are you going to be done?*	119
60. **dooy ni saai** *due to the nature*	120
61. **eeg noi** *soon*	121
62. **dooy tee** *such that*	122
63. **mun maak leuy!** *so much fun!*	123
64. **sa-roop waa** *so, to summarise*	124
65. **pood ngaai ngaai...** *to put it simply...*	125
66. **peua / peua tee ja** *for / in order to*	126
67. **(ao) wai kraao naa** *next time / no thanks / I'll pass*	127
68. **peua wai** *extra / just in case*	128
69. **mai dai tam / doo /** *etc. did not do / look / etc.*	129
70. **long meu (tam eng)** *hands on / do it yourself*	130
71. **lohk nee(-a)...** *(in) this world...*	131
72. **dtok jai / bplaek jai tee** *startled / shocked / surprised that...*	132
73. **mai hen duai** *don't agree*	134
74. **mai hen bpen bpan-haa** *that's not a problem / I don't see what the problem is*	135
75. **tam too-ra** *do errands / do 'stuff'*	136
76. **mai saduak** *not convenient / I would rather not*	138
77. **dee jung leuy** *great!*	140
78. **chawp bawk waa** *likes to say / often says*	141
79. **law len** *just kidding*	142
80. **wai jai mai daai** *cannot trust*	143
81. **baep / baep waa** *it's like*	144
82. **mae waa ja bpen** *no matter whether / what...*	145
83. **suan yai** *usually / normally*	146
84. **rawk** *no literal meaning*	147
85. **reuay reuay** *on and on / going ok / continuously*	148
86. **hetpon tee** *the reason that*	150
87. **krai bawk?** *who says?*	151
88. **na wan / dtawn nee** *as of today / now / as things stand*	152
89. **hai kao tam** *let him do / make him do / get him to do*	153
90. **reu mai gaw** *or if not then... / or otherwise...*	154
91. **mai roo dtua** *not aware*	155
92. **sia o-gaat / sia daai** *missed a chance / what a shame*	156
93. **mai mee je-dta-na...** *had no intention...*	157
94. **ngaw** *to win back the love of your loved one by apologizing...*	158
95. **gaan tee (rao ja...)** *the fact that...*	160
96. **nai tee soot** *in the end*	161
97. **chang mun teuh** *forget it / don't worry about it / leave it*	162
98. **prawm gup** *along with*	163
99. **diao** *wait / you wait and see / no literal meaning*	164
100. **mun sai!** *the feeling you have when you say "give me a break"*	166
Further Learning	168

NB: Transliteration above written without tone or other pronunciation marks.

PREFACE

- Can you say more than a few words in Thai or are you learning Thai?

- Do you find that taking Thai classes or reading Thai language books is not getting you very far?

- Are you able to communicate in only simple Thai sentences but want to be able to speak flexibly and at length and on more complex situations in everyday life?

- Do Thai people insist on replying to you in English even if you speak Thai with them?

- Do you get frustrated when you have to switch to English to explain what you mean?

- Do you find that in spite of all your lessons, the minute you listen to a Thai conversation you are lost? Do you find it hard to follow Thai TV, even interviews with 'daa-raa' and so on?

- Would you like to accelerate your Thai learning or simply get up to a level where you can converse comfortably?

- Do you want to 'sound' Thai (rather than a foreigner speaking basic Thai in 'a foreigner way')?

If you answered "Yes" to any of these eight questions, this book is for you.

What is "sounding Thai"?

The very first thing we need to do is to define what is sounding Thai and what is natural Thai and also, maybe more importantly, what they are not. Without this, the rest of the book will be meaningless because we will not know what we are aiming for in the first place. Let's define our terms of reference and objectives.

Sounding Thai and speaking natural Thai – what are these? Presumably the way 'real' Thai people speak? But who do we mean by these real Thai people? Do we mean younger 18 to 30 year old Bangkok people speaking Thai with their friends in cafes? Is it really that simple? Let's ask some questions to challenge this:

If those are the real Thai people then are Thai people over 60 not real? Their language is different to the younger generation in just the same way as e.g. English pensioners' to English young people's. I know my own English language has changed from 20 years ago when I was at university. I suspect your's has too.

And what about social class? If 'street Thai' is what we should aim for then what about upper class Thai? Are they not real Thai or natural? And what about so called working class Thai?

Then let's ask ourselves whether formal Thai such as spoken on TV and radio is not natural and speaking this means you do not sound Thai? What about Koon Saw-ra-yóot's Thai? What about about the Thai on 'Dtee Táai Krua'? What about Ca-ra-mae's Thai? Is it appropriate to learn so called natural Thai if it closely equates to street Thai and then use it with colleagues in the office? Or when speaking to a civil servant at a government office? Or even to a sales clerk?

Finally, let's also consider who is doing the learning here – foreigners to Thailand, right? Is it appropriate, or even possible, for foreigners to copy everything of a Thai person's speech? All the idioms, metaphors, implications, subtexts, social norms and cultural references and slang that Thais have grown up with?

Imagine a Thai person who can speak English to basic / intermediate standard saying "Yo bruv, yo mate, gi' us a fag mate. Cheers mate.". Now imagine that Thai person was a 70 year old woman from a wealthy family in Thailand. Is this the type of so called 'natural' English that is suitable for this person to learn in order to 'sound English'? Of course it is not.

Does all of this mean that it is impossible to even define what kind of Thai we should aim for? Are we beaten even before we have started? Fortunately, we can resort to common sense to focus our efforts and provide guidelines as to what is natural Thai?

What we have established so far is that the Thai that we aspire to as learners of Thai who want to speak Thai naturally depends on who the learners are i.e. their age, their 'class' etc, the context of the conversation, the situation and who the other party to the conversation is and finally, not forgetting that the person is a foreigner, not Thai and speaking Thai as a foreigner.

Clearly it is not feasible to write a book that caters for all of these parameters in every single combination. The best way to do this is be middle of the road – this approach will give you a solid and natural base from where you can tailor according to your set of circumstances. So neither too street, nor too posh, neither too teenage-y nor too 'old', neither too much slang nor too formal.

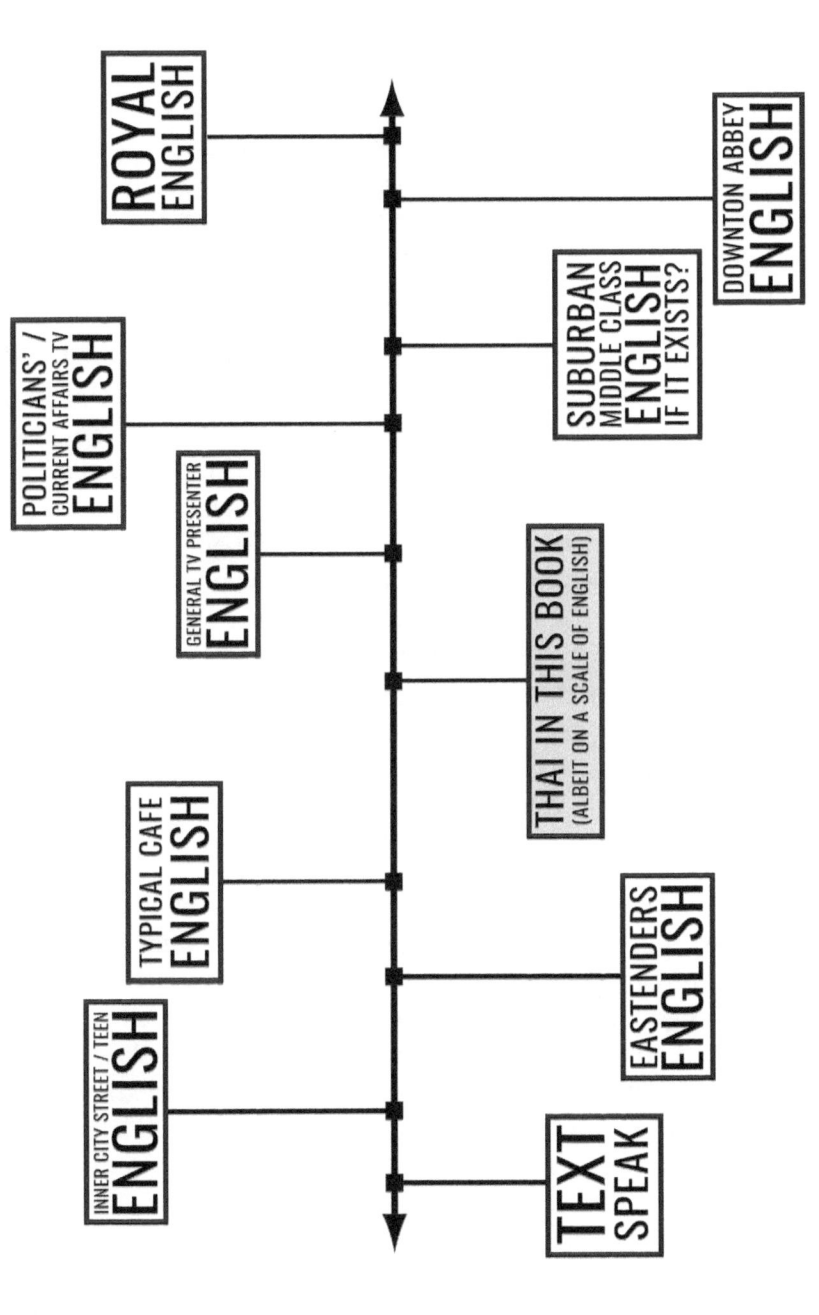

The diagram on the previous page is a representation of where different types of English may appear on a scale of formality (and loosely, age) and where the Thai in this book would appear if it were an English book. Obviously, I have used English on the scale because you can relate to this; once you become more familiar with all the different types and styles of Thai speech, you will be able to think of corresponding Thai points on the scale.

So, to return to the question of what is sounding Thai and what is speaking Thai naturally, the short answer is the Thai in this book, which is a good midpoint from where to develop your own age-appropriate, context-appropriate, social class-appropriate Thai. Bear in mind also that the minute you write any sentence down out of context outside of a conversation, it will sound less natural. So, no textbook, not even this one can ever represent a real conversation unless it contains actual transcripts of conversations. Since I do not want you to just use this book to copy phrases, I have not provided any actual conversations - the point is to learn the words and structures. Having said all of this, you can rest assured that the Thai in this book is more natural and close to real everyday speech than the textbooks out there.

And if you need any more convincing, this book has been edited and approved by **Kru Yuki**, a prominent and very well known Thai teacher who espouses natural Thai in her teaching. Kru Yuki has checked and advised on all the Thai in this book so you can be assured that this book will help you to speak natural Thai and sound Thai. And to repeat, don't fall into the trap of thinking that you should speak like a 25 year old girl chatting with her friends if you are a 65 year old man from California – that is not sounding Thai, it is sounding plain ridiculous. Now that we are clear on sounding Thai, let's move on.

What makes this book different?

The answer is simple – this book teaches you 100 Thai words that you should know and make you sound Thai. It will transform your spoken Thai to a level where you talk like a Thai person and are comfortable in using the language to speak at length, explain relatively complex subjects and situations and do it all in a natural style. This book gives you the words you need to form sentences for everyday use and therefore is a complement to books targeted at beginners, which give you the foundations – the basic nouns, verbs, adjectives, grammar rules etc. The words (of which most are phrases rather than single words) in this book are the missing link that will allow you to be confident speaking Thai.

- If you are a complete beginner, you will need a book on basic Thai to get the fundamentals down. However, if you want to, you can use this book to copy and practise some sentences in real life. Learning by study, interspersed with some real life attempts to speak, will provide balance and context. At beginner level, a bit of rote-learning can be useful to get up some confidence in speaking.

- If you are at a basic level, this book will help you quickly make use of the new words you already know and accelerate your learning of spoken Thai.

- If you can get by in Thai, this book will help you become fluent in everyday Thai.

- If you are already fluent in everyday spoken Thai, this book will firstly help you test yourself on whether you really are fluent – you may be surprised – and secondly, will allow you to develop richer and more rewarding conversations.

In my experience, many of the Thai language books available in the market are good and serve a necessary purpose to learn the fundamentals and basic vocabulary that you will need...BUT...the difference between the level you reach after going through these books and the reality of speaking Thai with confidence and at length is huge. The example sentences given in these books are rather rigid and hardly ever spoken as such in real life. Worst of all, reading and memorizing one example sentence only allows you to repeat that single sentence if a situation happens to demand it but how about if, rather than repeating out of a book "*Yes, I am hungry*"...in response to a question, you want to say:

"*Actually, I am a little bit hungry because I woke up late today and only had some cereal and then had to rush off to work and had no time to eat all day*"?

Can you say it in Thai? It is something you could and possibly would say naturally in English but even if you know a lot of the Thai nouns, verbs and adjectives from the above, would you struggle to form the sentence? This book will give you the missing ingredients that you need to make use of all the fundamentals that you may already be learning or have picked up along the way and start sounding natural in your spoken Thai.

And that is the inspiration behind this book. I learnt Thai from books myself, a couple of rather good books – **Teach yourself Thai** by **David Smyth** and **Essential Thai** by **James Higbie**. I noticed however that while there are plenty of books like these two (and none better I suspect), there are very few books for those who want to progress beyond these basic level books to more advanced books but still focused on conversational, 'normal' Thai. Most advanced books seem to be quite academic and old fashioned and contain Thai that is either too formal or too textbook-like to ever be used in real life. So if you had progressed beyond phrasebooks and beginner level books, what could you do without looking forward with a heavy heart to having to wade through a weighty textbook on Thai grammar and instructions on how to write Thai and so on. And so this book was born.

This book contains example sentences that are not the traditional, rigid, old fashioned and formal Thai that you will never be able to use in real life without sounding weird. Several of the examples are from my own life and experiences in Thailand. You will also notice that some example sentences are deliberately longer and more complex than the simple sentences you find in books targeted at beginners – there is no point in me filling this book with "I am from New York", "The weather is hot", "Which way is the toilet?" etc. Also you will notice that many sentences are not necessarily ones that you can readily copy – the idea is to learn **how** to use the words, not rote-learn.

I hope this book helps you transform your Thai to a whole new level. Later, I have expanded on how I learnt Thai. Hopefully, this will give you some insight into how to learn Thai yourself...and sound Thai! Good luck!!

By the way, the way I would say the sentence about being hungry, in Thai, could be:

Jing jing gâw hǐuw níd nòi práw wâa wan née dtèun sǎai láeo gin dtàe 'cerean' (cereal) dtawn cháao láeo gâw dtâwng rêep bpai tam ngaan; mâi mee we-laa gin a-rai èeg táng wan leuy.

จริง ๆ ก็หิวนิดหน่อยเพราะว่าวันนี้ตื่นสาย แล้วกินแต่ 'ซีเรียล' ตอนเช้า แล้วก็ต้องรีบไปทำงานไม่มีเวลากินอะไรอีกทั้งวันเลย

ABOUT THE AUTHOR

I am from the UK (which Thai people rarely believe because I am from Bangladesh in terms of my ethnic origin, which is what they are really asking me when they ask where I am from!) and born and brought up in London. I first went to Thailand on a short business trip, sent by my very first employer – a banking technology company. As with most first time visitors, I was enchanted by Thailand and wanted to return asap. I got myself a book – **Essential Thai** by **James Higbie**, the best basic Thai book out there in my opinion – and started learning at home in London. Following two short holidays to Thailand over the next two years, where I used every chance to practise the Thai I had learnt in my books, I got the chance to work in the Thai branch for three years. Within two years I was fluent.

To qualify my fluency, I should state from the off that I am by no means bilingual / native proficiency. I am not a Thai teacher per se and I have no god given talent as a linguist and I could not be a Thai interpreter or read a Thai newspaper and I do not study Thai as a profession or even a hobby. I still (albeit rarely) mispronounce or lazy-pronounce (where you know the tone but don't make the effort to deviate from mid-tone) words. So I am not an 'expert' and I make no claim to be a Thai language guru or professor.

However I am fluent in Thai, which means I can speak at length with a friend on my childhood, or with a taxi driver on the state of Thailand, or with a tradesman on the dangers and attraction of casinos and why Thailand is better off without one, or go through my CV in detail with a recruitment agent in Thai, to give some random examples. And I can live in Thailand speaking entirely in Thai with friends, shop staff etc. Most importantly, I sound (almost) Thai.

And to qualify that last point about not sounding Thai completely, even if you are in Thai academia or study Thai to expert level on a long term basis (and I am guessing the vast majority of you are not and do not intend to be), you will never sound 100% Thai (or should expect to). As you become familiar with Thai, you will see that there is a huge tendency to economise on words in Thai and use lots of implication and you may not get away with speaking like that. That's why you find it hard to follow two Thai people talking in many informal situations.

Think about how you speak English (or your native language) and compare to how foreigners to your country speak your language, even the ones that are very good...they still don't speak like you, right? In many cases, foreigners speak **more** correctly than native speakers, who take liberties with pronunciation, formality, grammar and so on because it is their own language. Thai is the same. So my aim is to get you from textbook Thai to comfortable spoken Thai at a level where you can converse with Thai people naturally, without they having to slow down too much for you but recognizing that your conversations still won't sound 100% exactly like two Thai people talking. Which is absolutely fine – just try to get ever closer to 100%. Got it?

Note that being able to answer questions on where you are from, how old you are, how long you have been in Thailand, what you had for dinner and so on does NOT mean you are fluent, it means you are between basic and intermediate level. In general, responding to questions, especially these obvious questions, is a lot easier than having to create your own thoughts and questions in a foreign language and maintain a conversation or respond with more than just the minimum response learnt in a book. BTW, when I say intermediate, I mean your comfort with everyday spoken Thai and the complexity of what you can say BUT still within the scope of normal everyday situations. So, I do not mean intermediate = talking about global warming and advanced is discussing Thai politics in detail. I am assuming most of you will not be doing any of this and if you do, you are already studying Thai formally. This book is all about the words that get you to fluency in non-formal, everyday situational Thai, which I hope caters for the majority of you.

Below I have given a very detailed list of things I did to learn Thai. I am sure you all have your own methods so if you want to stick to your method, no problem but if you are interested, the tips below could help you learn faster.

What specific things I did to learn to speak Thai quickly and to try to sound Thai (and things you should do if you are serious about learning Thai)

Probably the most important point is I had the motivation. Without this, you will never achieve fluency or speak Thai as Thai people do. You need to have an overriding drive and desire to learn Thai! Whether it is because of falling in love, or a job in a company or location where English is not commonly spoken or any other clear reason to learn Thai, this reason is paramount.

Secondly, as a direct consequence of the first point, I tried really, really hard! I am not a linguist and I do not pick up languages within days as multi-lingual people may do. So I did the following things which illustrate the lengths I went to to try and learn.

- I read my books over and over again and then again and then again. I cross-referenced books to get two or more perspectives on the same word or grammar rule or whatever.

- I did not jump to trying to remember basic sentences too quickly. I spent a lot of time studying the excellent explanations of the grammar basics and pronunciation rules in James Higbie's (and I am sure many other) book i.e. the consonants that do not directly correspond to an English consonant, the vowel sounds, the tones, how to pronounce words starting with 'ng' and so on.

- I focused on speaking first, reading second and not at all on writing. Why? I have no use for writing Thai and given a limited number of hours I could spend after work and on weekends studying, I needed to make a decision on how best to direct this effort to the most valuable skill. I did study how to read, to an extent, because it does help in pronunciation and understanding of the language. So I can read to a basic level by remembering words that I have read before, as opposed to being able to spell. The difference? If I come across a word I have never read before, I would not know what tone it is because I did not properly learn which class of letter and tone mark combination creates which tone. The tone rules are not all that complicated so this was just a personal choice.

    ◦ To qualify further – I know one or two Thai learners who spend huge amounts of effort on reading books and learning to write Thai script, chat on Thai forums but the minute they start talking, it is obvious they are barely above basic proficiency. Sometimes these learners sound simply awful to a Thai ear but they manage to get through because the meaning is often obvious from the context of the situation and because of the Thais' legendary accommodating disposition. And so, these foreigners go through their stay in Thailand, often many years, speaking bad Thai and maybe believing that they are fluent. They have all the grammar rules, the vocabulary, the ability to spell but they do not sound natural or worse still, cannot string together all the words they know to express what they really mean.

- My view was clear from the start – focus on speaking. Listen very carefully to how Thai sounds and copy. Ignore trying to write Thai (unless, of course, I had had the time and willpower and need to learn to write). I want to help you be fluent first and foremost. I encourage you to get out there and speak as much as you can and even more important, listen!! Then, listen again!!!

- Finally, notice that I did NOT say learn **by** speaking first; I said learn **to** speak first. As I said at the start of this section I learned by reading my book over and over again. So, don't misunderstand – you need to study to get a basic level of knowledge and comfort in order to speak but don't keep reading forever and forget to practise. That's the point. And leave writing till later.

- I read up on a word and then, at work the next day, I deliberately tried to steer conversations toward that word so that I could use it in a sentence I had made up myself and test colleagues' reaction. This is one of the most important things that I suggest you do if you really want to learn. You need to have the drive and planning effort to prepare like this and the focus to ensure you somehow get into a conversation where you can test out your word at some point in the day. It takes that much effort.

- I noted their reaction and asked where I had gone wrong and jotted, either mentally or in a notebook, what I had learnt and then went back to my book to check I had understood the point.

- I deliberately tried to start conversations with everyone around me – taxi drivers (a great choice), shop assistants, massage therapists etc. I was not afraid to ask if I had said it correctly, which often led to even more confusion but I persevered.

- I tried to read street signs, menus, karaoke subtitles, translations of Thai songs on websites and asked Thai people (politely) when I could not read a word on a street sign or menu etc.

- I noted when I had attempted to say a Thai word e.g. at a coffee shop ordering some food, and I received confusion so had clearly mispronounced or misunderstood. I realized that it was my fault, not the listener's and so it was me who needed to change and improve, not the listener. Perhaps I had got the tone wrong or perhaps I forgot to put the verb at the end or maybe I just said it in a way that no Thai person would – the point was it must have meant that I was wrong and therefore, I needed to go back and work on it again. (Note, there are some rare occasions when you do speak perfectly but the fact that the listener is so shocked that you can speak Thai, they forget to listen and so do not understand and give you the confused look).

- I listened to (and genuinely liked) Thai songs from bands and artists such as Bodyslam, Big Ass, Clash, Dunk Punkorn, Blackhead, Potato, Labanoon and so on.

- I watched Thai TV and asked when I wanted to learn a specific word i.e. "what was that word she said just then... sounded like 'tamada'"? "Kum năi....aaaw...tam-ma-daa châi mái...mun bplae wâa 'normal'".

- Like most people, I found the tones difficult and so, when I got a word wrong because of the tone, I would go back and use my book to mentally score the look of that word written in transliterated Thai into my brain. To this day, this is the way I can pronounce tones – I remember what the word looks like typed in a book including the tone mark. If you have actually learnt the tone rules properly, that's even better obviously.

- And probably one of the most critical keys to my 'success' in achieving fluency, as I have stressed several times already, I listened! I listened to every Thai conversation around me and I paid attention! I did not just allow the sounds to wash over me or go in one ear and out the other. I paid attention. I jotted down sounds that to my ears approximated to an interesting word, or maybe the only word out of a sentence that I did not understand, or maybe if I had heard the same word more than twice in a day. I would then find a way to ask or use my dictionary or whatever to work out what word my phonetic jotting actually was. Again, it takes that much effort…yes, it does.

- And most importantly, I listened to how Thai sounded, where people would emphasise a syllable, the difference in accents, common words and common responses that I heard over and over again and so on. I then ensured I copied these sounds so that when I tried to speak, I did not sound like I was speaking Thai with an English accent. This is a lot harder to do than it sounds because it can be embarrassing to go outside of your comfort zone and make sounds that are alien to your native language but this is absolutely crucial to speaking Thai like a Thai person. So go ahead, don't be shy, copy what you hear. Let go of English and pronounce it the way you hear it, not the closest approximation to an English sound.

I hope my story and the tips above have inspired you to learn Thai with an aim to at least be fluent. This will not only make your life in Thailand a little easier, understanding and speaking Thai will allow you to truly appreciate Thai people, culture, attitudes, behaviour and make your stay in Thailand immeasurably more fulfilling. So I urge you to use this book to springboard your learning and enjoy Thailand – one of the greatest countries in the world.

INTRODUCTION

This book contains a list of words and phrases that will help to transform your ability to communicate in Thai from a basic level to intermediate and beyond. While many newcomers to Thai can successfully memorise the basics – colours, foods, basic directions, say that food is tasty – they often find it difficult to understand everyday spoken Thai.

The main reason for this is that knowing a set of nouns, adjectives and verbs by itself only goes so far and there are a set of linking words, context / time-setting words, common expressions, and so on, that are necessary for basic speakers to know in order to start conversing with confidence. Note also that the example sentences given here are not the usual formal, rigid sentences that you may see in most Thai language books; again, in reality nobody speaks in textbook language and so the examples attempt to reflect a more natural spoken style. Try to find situations to practise these words and phrases with Thai people and see your conversations becoming richer and more fulfilling.

This book actually teaches a lot more than the 100 words in the title of the book. I have used the format of a list of 100 words to not just explain the word itself but also most of the other interesting words and phrases in the example sentences, thus breaking out into three, four or more words or clauses and explaining these. This allows you to build up a significant set of vocabulary and ways of expression far beyond just the 100 words to build your confidence in Thai. And there are also tips and insights into many of the words. Taken together, these features mean that this book is your invaluable guide on how to go from basic to intermediate level, and beyond, in normal, conversational Thai.

Before we get going with the main part of the book, I want to return to the topic of sounding Thai one more time as it is central to this book and also your credibility as a Thai speaker. First, as I have explained previously, you will never sound 100% Thai and that is just fine. Most of the 'street' Thai or young person's Thai that you hear around you is certainly good to know and even use yourself on occasion and it will get you closer to sounding Thai but you simply do not have the cultural background and social norms that a native speaker has grown up with to sound 100% Thai. And that is just fine. And as I said before, a native speaker will often speak **less** accurately, or expressively, or clearly, or directly, than you so it is not the case that the more Thai you know, the more you sound Thai. Native speakers can take all sorts of liberties with their expression because it is their own language – if you listen to your own English, I bet you would not find any book that teaches people to speak English like you do.

Having said all the above, you can and should try to get ever closer to 100% sounding Thai, which I define as native speaker Thai, which is beyond fluency. This book helps you to get to fluency and gives you the foundations to go beyond fluency to sounding Thai. And that means having a balance between 'street Thai', Thai suitable to your age and social status and formal Thai. Just as in the Queen's English, there is a concept of correct Thai so don't think sounding Thai = 'street' Thai. Get the balance right.

Finally, as well as learning these 100 words, please, please, please do NOT speak Thai with an English / American accent! All your hard work learning the words is totally undone and your credibility shot to pieces if you do not say the words in the accent of the language. Listen hard and copy the sounds and rhythms of Thai; importantly, men, don't copy all your speech from women!

KEY FEATURES OF THIS BOOK

I have already expanded in the previous section on how I learnt Thai so to summarise...memorizing words and sentences and practising them on native speakers and seeing their reaction etc. is the first step only. The real key to making progress is being able to combine elements of one or several example sentences given in this book to say what you want, to fit your own situation. Want an example? Instead of saying "*I like Thailand*" when asked what you think about the country, why not say "Actually (jing jing) I like Thailand...if I compare (tâa pǒm tîap) my life here to back home, it seems like (mun měuan gùp wâa), I am happier (more content – sà-baai jai gwàa) here". See?

Note that this book does not teach pronunciation in detail, which again, I have left to your existing Thai learning books. I am assuming you know by now that pronunciation, especially when it comes to Thai, is paramount. If you are shaky on your tones and 'odd' sounding Thai alphabet, you should continuously try to improve in those areas alongside all the new sentences you will be saying using this book. Crucially, listen to how Thai people speak.

To speak Thai the way Thai people do, as a basic level learner, you need to think of what you want to say in English - the nouns, verbs and / or adjectives – and then pick out the supporting words in this book to make it a natural sounding sentence. Or, take something that you normally say or have read in a book and try adding one or two words to it from the 100 words in this book and test it out on a native speaker. As you become more advanced and can create your own sentences, or even better, think in Thai, you are well on your way to fluency!

Slang – Note that this book does not teach Thai slang and most of the words (with one or two exceptions) in this book are not slang. You may assume reading this far that I am espousing the dumbing-down of Thai and nothing is further from the truth. I am absolutely not recommending you to speak bad Thai or slang; the majority of this book is colloquial Thai of a fairly balanced nature – neither too posh nor too 'street'. Once you understand Thai and Thailand enough, you can make your own judgement on where you fit on the spectrum, which may be based on your perception of your own class, social circle, the context of the majority of your conversations (work, bar, academia etc). Until you are that good, I do not think it wise to teach you a very formal, text book like language that you will neither hear often nor be able to, or more importantly, need to reproduce. Ok?

It is advisable to not use slang when you do not yet have a comprehensive grasp of the language; at best, you may use slang inappropriately and at worst, cause offence and that goes double for swear words or other words one may have picked up in Thailand's nightlife scene. Even if you get lots of laughs with your ability to repeat words you have picked up on the street, trust me, those are polite, nervous laughs and you are not doing yourself any favours. Thai people are very good at not revealing their true thoughts so do not be fooled by your increased popularity when you turn up and say "a-rai wâh??!!" and get a round of laughs. Stick to the words in this book until you are fluent. Once you sound Thai, you have 'earned the right' to be more creative and sometimes using slang is acceptable and doesn't sound weird, as it would if you can only speak basic Thai but confidently mix in slang. Think how ridiculous foreigners to UK / US sound when they are good at slang but can barely speak English.

Note that most examples I have given in this book are written without the 'krúp' or 'kà' at the end. I am sure you know that you need to add these in real life when you speak, especially when you are directing your words at someone such as requesting something or responding to a question. In fact, to an extent, using these particles will mitigate any grammatical mistakes you make in your speech because you will still sound polite to a Thai ear.

In addition to defining the 100 words, the context, defining many of the other words of note and example sentences, I have included a set of tips and insights into some of the words, sometimes using my own experiences in Thailand. Hopefully this will help.

INDICATOR ICONS TO CONVEY NUANCE

And to make things more interesting / fun, I have provided some extra insight into some words by using a set of indicator icons and strength ratings alongside (2 of the indicators). Ratings are on a scale of 1 to 5, with 1 being the mildest form of the indicator and 5, the strongest form.

So, a word with a Bluntness indicator and a 3 rating means it is quite a direct expression but not aggressive or rude. A Feminine indicator of 5 suggests it is a word that is really only used by women but can be used by men if they are doing it deliberately or ironically. Ultimately, there are no hard and fast rules – these are just to give you insight into the feel of the language.

There are five indicator icons in total and they are:

 FEMININE INDICATOR

 BLUNTNESS INDICATOR

 INDIRECTNESS INDICATOR

 SOFTNESS INDICATOR

 'THAI-NESS' INDICATOR

'Feminine' indicator – This highlights words that are mainly (if given a 5 rating) used by women, or where pronouncing a word in a certain way makes it sound more feminine. As a general rule, the more emotional, expressive, flamboyant or prima-donna like your language sounds, just as with English, the more feminine it will sound. In Thailand, with fairly traditional gender roles and a strong gay culture, sounding 'manly' (if you are a man) is a little more relevant than in the West. Since many Western men tend to spend time interacting more with Thai women (and have few Thai male friends), they tend to pick up words and tones that are effeminate. One quick example – some male foreigners pick up the female practice of referring to yourself by name instead of "I" – men, don't do it, especially in formal situations!

Of course nobody will take you to trial if you are male and your general speech is a little feminine in sound but people may be mildly amused and give each other a knowing smile when they hear you say words that you maybe picked up from your wife or female colleagues. And being a foreigner means your speech (and other behaviour) is more open to judgement, unlike native speakers. On the other hand, if you are skilled enough, you can even deliberately pronounce words in a feminine way to get a laugh or break the ice. For female readers, there are no real equivalents (apart from swearing, which is seen as more of a male characteristic) so ladies speak freely!

 Bluntness indicator – Where a word gives a hint of bluntness or even in rare cases, aggressiveness to the overall meaning. Most of the words here are 1s and 2s; a 5 would be verging on outright rudeness or swearing.

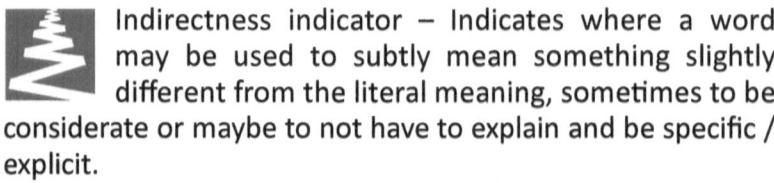 Indirectness indicator – Indicates where a word may be used to subtly mean something slightly different from the literal meaning, sometimes to be considerate or maybe to not have to explain and be specific / explicit.

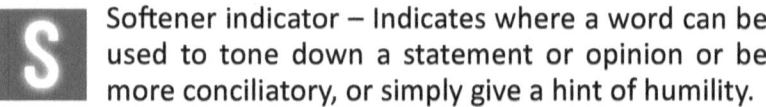 Softener indicator – Indicates where a word can be used to tone down a statement or opinion or be more conciliatory, or simply give a hint of humility. These are two of the key concepts in Thai i.e. speaking in a way that does not offend others or make them lose face or create an uncomfortable situation. Unlike Western culture where directness and assertiveness are virtues, Thai is more about consideration for others and being humble.

Using softeners and indirectness separates you from those who may well be able to speak accurately but maybe not naturally. Your sentences will still be accurate without these but you will not fully fit into Thai society without them and at worst, may come off as boorish. In many cases, these words can also be your saviour as your opinion of something may be misguided or due to a lack of understanding of Thai culture so softening your displeasure will allow you to save face when you realize you were wrong!

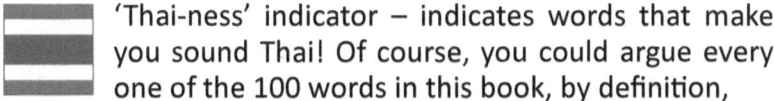 'Thai-ness' indicator – indicates words that make you sound Thai! Of course, you could argue every one of the 100 words in this book, by definition, make you sound Thai because they are of the Thai language! But the point here is to highlight the words that have that extra something special that perhaps Thai people would not necessarily expect you to know and may be pleasing to a Thai ear. Some of these words do not have a direct translation into English hence increasing the 'Thai-ness' factor, while others are words that Thai people use naturally in everyday language and would not assume a foreigner would learn in a book. Some of these words may even be superfluous to the meaning of a given sentence but often these words make the difference between someone who speaks a language based on rigid, studied effort and one who has naturally picked up the language and blends into society smoothly. Like I said, I could have designated all 100 with this indicator but have tried to pick the best words for you to impress...and so have ignored some of the more abrupt words, even if they have 'Thai-ness'.

CULTURAL TIPS AND INSIGHT

As well as all of the above, I have also included a set of cultural insights that you may find useful. As you will see, in keeping with my non traditional Thai language book approach, the cultural insights are also not the usual ones you see on Thai websites or in books. I have attempted to give you the kind of insight you only get from living in Thailand. By no means am I suggesting the traditional tips are wrong; my tips simply add to these to give you extra insight and understanding of things you may encounter in your life in Thailand.

TRANSLITERATION AND GUIDE TO PRONUNCIATION

This book assumes you have a basic understanding of the tones, the consonants and vowels, the pronunciation rules and the transliteration rules you have come across in your books already. I do not plan to provide a comprehensive breakdown of all of this and will leave you to rely on your existing knowledge and also check out **James Higbie**'s excellent book – **Essential Thai** – for a comprehensive guide to transliteration and pronunciation. Also, I do not want to put you off learning Thai by giving you a huge breakdown of all the pronunciation rules – I have to admit, I did go through them, spending hours and hours learning and memorizing but not everyone has that kind of patience. As long as you realize pronunciation is important in a tonal language, don't let it stop you.

So for the purposes of this book, I have provided below a summary of the method I have used and some pronunciation basics. I have not gone through every single consonant and vowel and tone as that would require several pages and I am hoping you are already familiar with these from elsewhere. Indeed, you really should spend a significant amount of time getting the pronunciation rules drummed into your head before you go too far into your learning. Conversely, do not let the difficulty of pronunciation put you off – yes, you will mis-pronounce a lot initially but you may still be understood from the context and you are far better off trying, failing and then asking where you mis-pronounced than spending forever learning to read and write but unable to hold a basic conversation.

Tones and vowel length

Long syllables have no '_' while short syllables will always have an '_' underneath. Double vowels indicate longer sounds but the '_' always takes precedence. Therefore, 'tóok' is a shorter, more stunted sound; even though it is a double vowel, the underline takes precedence and shortens the sound. Conversely, 'bprà-têt' only has a single 'e' but is a longer 'e' sound like 'get' but holding the 'e' for longer — "geeet outta my way". Hyphenated words are to show the syllable breakdown, not to indicate a pause in pronunciation.

There are five tones in Thai — medium or monotone, lòw, hígh, rǐsing (like "oh yeeaah??") and fâlling ("oh nooo!!").

Consonants

Dt – this is a sound between a 'd' and 't' i.e. a soft 't', like 'style' but softer with the tip of the tongue under the front teeth, which is different to both 'day' and 'table'.

Bp – this is a sound between a 'b' and 'p', like 'suppose', which is different to 'bread' and 'party'.

Vowels

There are short and long versions of most vowels. I have not listed every single one of these because in most cases, the double vowelled transliteration will make it obvious and, as discussed above, the underlines always take precedence and are the definitive indicator of short sounds.

A – as in 'Obama'. Note that I use 'a' in most cases but in some cases, 'u' for the same 'car' sound.

Ae – as in the first and third 'a' in 'caravan'

O – as in 'go', not 'pot'; longer version spelt with an h – 'mohng'

Aw – as in 'Squawk' (slight American accent to bring the lower jaw down)

Ooy – as in 'loiter' (posh English accent) but slightly elongated, rounded 'o'

U – as in 'fun', not 'rude' when it is a 'u' by itself; when it is part of a combination vowel such as 'ua', 'ui' or 'uay', it is 'u' as in 'rude'.

Eu – as in "err…what do you mean?"

Oi – as in 'Aw' above with a 'y' sound at the end; 'Ooi' is more elongated

~~Eu~~ – no real equivalent in English but the closest is 'dude' (like in all the LA teen films) said with a smile and the mouth stretched out. Elongated sound. Best way…practise saying "p̌ǒm chêu̶…" (*"my name is…"*) with a Thai person.

There are many more vowels and vowel combinations but I am hoping most of these should be obvious from the transliteration and if not, do reference the plethora of material on this topic online and in books.

Spoken language spelling

One final principle that I have tried to adhere to in this book is to spell transliterated words as they are pronounced in real life. Of course, the vast majority of words are spelt the same in written and spoken Thai but there are a few words where this is not the case. For these few, in being consistent with my emphasis on spoken Thai, I have spelt the transliteration of these few words as they are said rather than spelt, while the Thai script is still written as it should be written in written script. Don't worry, the difference in tone or vowel length is very minimal anyway and, as you will see with all of the below, the reason for the difference is the spoken version is easier to say and doesn't adversely affect the rhythm of the words.

'<u>yàng</u>' (as in '<u>yàng</u> née' – '*like this*' is a short sound when speaking at full speed even though it is spelt in Thai with a long 'aa'. When slowing down to enunciate, it is said slightly longer but still not as long as '<u>yaang</u>' – '*rubber*'.

'<u>yàng</u> née / <u>nán</u>' is sometimes written as '<u>yàng</u> ngée / <u>ngán</u>' as is said in conversation – I use both in this book.

'<u>dâai</u>' is a long sound in this book when it is at the end of a sentence to mean '*can*' but when it precedes a verb to change it to past tense it is pronounced as a short sound and so will be written as '<u>dâi</u>' as in '<u>mâi</u> <u>dâi</u> <u>bpai</u>'.

Finally, '<u>chán</u>' – '*I*', '<u>mái</u>' – '*ending of a question*' and '<u>káo</u>' – '*he / she*' are all spelt with a high tone in the transliteration in this book even though they are written with a rising tone in the strictly correct written Thai form because the spoken versions of these words are all said with a high tone.

100 THAI WORDS THAT MAKE YOU SOUND THAI

1. a-<u>rai</u> <u>yàng</u> née(-<u>a</u>) อะไรอย่างนี้(อ่ะ)

Meaning – something like that / etc

Context – '<u>a</u>-<u>rai</u> <u>yàng</u> née-<u>a</u>' is often used at the end of a sentence when you describe something but do not want to list every single example of your point so for convenience, you can say '<u>a</u>-<u>rai</u> <u>yàng</u> née-<u>a</u>'. Note that '<u>a</u>-<u>rai</u> <u>yàng</u> née-<u>a</u>' is a fairly 'feminine' word but can be used by men, albeit trying to not emphasise the '-<u>a</u>' in too high pitched a tone…as women may do, closer to a '<u>ya</u>'. An alternative is '<u>a</u>-<u>rai</u> <u>yàng</u> <u>nán</u>'.

Example:

We-laa wâang, châwp <u>bpai</u> deuhn hâang, nûad <u>tai</u>….<u>a</u>-<u>rai</u> <u>yàng</u> née(<u>ya</u>)…<u>a</u>-<u>rai</u> têe 'relak' (relax) <u>nòi</u>.

เวลาว่าง ชอบไปเดินห้าง นวดไทย อะไรอย่างนี้ (อ่ะ) อะไรที่ 'รีแลกซ์' หน่อย

When I'm free, I like doing relaxing things like hanging out at malls, getting a massage…stuff like that.

Notice that in the above sentence, I have omitted '<u>pǒm</u>' in two places where it would have been in English speech – before and after '<u>wâang</u>'. Omission of pronouns where it is obvious who the speaker is talking about is a fundamental concept in Thai and takes some getting used to for foreigners.

Also notice the '<u>nòi</u>' at the end used as a softener or rather, to make the sentence more polite. which is, again, very common; ending the sentence without it would seem slightly abrupt.

<u>Wan</u> née <u>bpai</u> hăa măw. Măw bàwk wâa <u>bpen</u> <u>wàt</u>; <u>hâi</u> púk pàwn <u>yéuh</u> <u>yéuh</u>, hâam àwk <u>gam</u>-<u>lang</u> gaai, <u>a</u>-<u>rai</u> <u>yàng</u> née.

วันนี้ไปหาหมอ หมอบอกว่าเป็นหวัดให้พักผ่อน เยอะ ๆ ห้ามออกกำลังกาย อะไรอย่างนี้

Today I went to see the doctor. He said I have got a cold and told me to get lots of rest, no physical exercise and so on.

Did you notice the use of '<u>yéuh</u> <u>yéuh</u>'? Adjectives are often doubled to retain the rhythm of a sentence or to emphasise the point. It is one of those things that you develop as you get a better feel for the language.

> **Cultural insight / life in Thailand: Go with the flow**
>
> *Thailand can be a confusing place for foreigners. On the one hand it is certainly true that there will always be people who will look to take advantage of you and your perceived wealth. On the other hand you have been told and know from your own instincts that most people are well meaning and are happy to help you. So who do you trust and how do you navigate life in Thailand?*
>
> *Well, you use common sense and you try to learn as much as you can about your new surroundings and people's motivations. But don't let your wariness ruin your time in Thailand.*
>
> *When you are new to Thailand going with the flow is often the best way. When people suggest places to eat, what to order and so on, take a back seat and be led. You will be the beneficiary. Yes, there may be underlying reasons why people recommend certain things to you e.g. a certain tradesman but it does not mean that that reason is necessarily malicious. The tradesman could be the local guy and by using him you are simply supporting the local community. Even if he is a few baht more expensive, that is probably far outweighed by the hassle you would have trying to find cheaper.*

2. dtâng dtàe / dtâng naan / dtâng lăai kráng
ตั้งแต่   ตั้งนาน   ตั้งหลายครั้ง

Meaning – since / for a long time / many times

Context – 'dtâng' can be used in several ways; in the simplest way, 'dtâng dtàe' just means '*since*' but 'dtâng' can also be to precede indications of time that have passed e.g. a number of years. The reason for adding the 'dtâng' to '*many years*' or similar is to intensify the expression such as when you want to say you something has been planned for many years with no progress or when something is done many times with no success i.e. a sense of frustration. This use can come off as slightly 'feminine'.

Example:

Mâi dâi glàp bpai dtâng dtàe kào bplìan 'may-noo' (menu); yàak bpai měuan gun.

ไม่ได้กลับไปตั้งแต่เขาเปลี่ยน 'เมนู' อยากไปเหมือนกัน

Yeah, I wanted to go too, I haven't been back since they changed their menu.

Here is the past tense in Thai – the use of 'mâi dâi' turns the verb into something that happened in the past, or rather, to be more precise, the above is actually the present perfect tense. 'dâai' means '*to get*' and so 'mâi dâi' means '*I haven't gotten / didn't get to...*'. You can add it in front of other verbs like 'kíd' to mean you didn't think and so on.

Also notice that it is the 'dtâng dtàe' that actually makes this into a present perfect form of the verb, whereas the 'mâi dâi' by itself would just make it a past tense verb e.g. 'aa-tít têe laéo pǒm mâi dâi bpai tam ngaan' – '*I didn't go to work last week*'.

Finally, notice that if you wanted to state the past tense for something you did do (as opposed to did not), you do not have to add anything in front of the verb because it is obvious from the context of last week so 'aa-tít têe laéo (pǒm) bpai...' – you do not have to learn all the tense forms of verbs in Thai.

Mâi dâi jeuh náwng chaai dtâng lǎai bpee.

ไม่ได้เจอน้องชายตั้งหลายปี

I haven't seen my younger brother for many years.

Tam dtâng lǎai kráng dtàe yang mâi bprà-sòp kwaam sǎm-rèd leuy.

ทำตั้งหลายครั้ง แต่ยังไม่ประสบความสำเร็จเลย

I have done it / tried many times but still haven't had any success.

Learn to use the word 'dtàe ' – it is used in exactly the same way as in English so it should be easy to make up sentences in your head to practise with native speakers. For example, say something is good but then point out a less positive aspect of that thing and vice versa – the weather is good but it is rather hot or in England it rains a lot but you don't mind it much and so on.

3. tĕung máe wâa / tĕung yàng nán / tĕung káo jà
ถึงแม้ว่า ถึงอย่างนั้น ถึงเขาจะ

Meaning – even though / even if it is like that or in spite of that / even if he is going to

Context – this is a very useful word when you want to insist on something or want to state sentiments based on '*in spite of...*'. Often it is shortened to just 'tĕung'.

Example:

Tĕung yàng nán pŏm yang châwp rót BMW yòo dee.

ถึงอย่างนั้นผมยังชอบรถ บีเอ็มดับเบิ้นยู อยู่ดี

Even then / even if that is true, I still like BMW cars.

Notice the 'yòo dee' used at the end of the sentence. If you were to say this sentence in an English style, you would omit this phrase because the use of 'yang' already conveys the concept of '*still*' liking BMW cars so there is no need in English to add the 'yòo dee'. However in Thai, it is customary to include this type of ending to give the sentence the appropriate cadence it requires. In terms of meaning, as you may know, adding 'yòo' to a verb makes it continuous and so it can be seen that 'yòo dee' does not add much to the meaning but is there for cadence purposes.

Tĕung káo mâi soŏng káo gâw yang lên 'baat' (basketball) gèng.

ถึงเขาไม่สูง เขาก็ยังเล่น'บาส'เก่ง

Even though he is short, he is still really good at basketball.

As with 'relak' and 'baat' here, there are many words in Thai that are taken from English and pronounced in a Thai way just as there are many English words that are taken from, for example, French such as custard or alliance etc. Although it can be quite frustrating, you have to pronounce these words in the Thai way, not as you would in English EVEN IF they are English words absorbed into Thai. So there is no point saying 'relax' because words do not end with an 's' sound in Thai, or saying 'computer' in an English way – it is more like 'kawm-bpiu-dtêuh' with the second bit extended out. It may sound silly and unnecessary but think about foreign words absorbed into English and not pronounced as they are in their country of origin – this is no different. Finally, notice the abbreviation of 'basketball' – a common feature of Thai is to shorten words to one syllable for convenience, another subtlety to appreciate.

> **Cultural insight / life in Thailand: Land of smiles**
>
> *Thailand is well known around the world as the Land of Smiles, right? To the casual observer and certainly to tourists this seems to be the truth. And for the most part it actually is true; most people, including myself, who come back after visiting Thailand the first time will tell stories of the wonderful people and the amazing customer service and so on.*
>
> *But just bear in mind that Thai people are actually no different to any other people in terms of their basic human make-up and so they certainly don't spend all day smiling. Because most situations foreigners find themselves in contact with Thai people are a customer to seller / host situation, it is easy to assume Thais smile all the time. Also bear in mind that often Thais smile when they do not quite understand or to save you face when they are actually angry.*
>
> *None of the above takes away from the fact that Thai people are some of the most genuinely nice and welcoming people you will ever meet but as you stay longer in Thailand, try to be more aware of your own actions and how you come across – is it a real smile or is it bemusement or embarrassment on your behalf due to something you said or did?*

4. měuan gun เหมือนกัน

Meaning – the same as each other / also / agree

Context – although the literal meaning is '*the same as each other*', this word can be used in several ways. For example, it can be used to say that you agree with someone ('*think the same as each other*'), want to also watch the same movie and so on. Sometimes, 'měuan gun' is used in a similar way to '*I have to admit…*' in English or to soften the opinion.

Example:

Châi kíd měuan gun.

ใช่ คิดเหมือนกัน

Yes, I agree.

Mâi róo měuan gun.

ไม่รู้เหมือนกัน

(I have to admit) I don't know or I don't know either.

Mâi châi, mun mâi měuan gun; doo dee jà hěn kwaam dtáek dtaang.

ไม่ใช่มันไม่เหมือนกัน ดูดี ๆ จะเห็นความแตกต่าง

No, they're not the same; if you look carefully, you'll see the dif-ferences.

5. tâa <u>yàng nán</u> / <u>ngún</u> ถ้าอย่างนั้น / งั้น

Meaning – in that case

Context – just as in English, this is a useful phrase when deciding on something or giving an opinion, given a situation or set of facts. Note that '<u>ngún</u>' is just an abbreviation and there are several other examples of 'yang...something' being abbreviated to just 'ng...' such as "<u>yang ngai</u>" to '<u>ngai</u>'.

Example:

Person A: <u>Wan</u> née <u>rót</u> <u>jà</u> <u>dtìd</u> <u>práw</u> <u>bpen</u> <u>wan</u> <u>sòok</u>. Person B: <u>Ngún</u> <u>pǒm</u> kuan <u>jà</u> <u>chái</u> <u>rót</u> <u>fai</u>-fáa dee gwàa <u>châi</u> <u>mái</u>?

คนแรก: วันนี้ รถจะติด เพราะเป็นวันศุกร์ คนที่สอง: งั้นผมควรจะใช้รถไฟฟ้าดีกว่าใช่ไหม

Person A: Today the traffic is going to be really bad because it is Friday. Person B: In that case it's better for me to take the skytrain, right?

'<u>rót</u> <u>dtìd</u>' is a very common topic of conversation in Thailand as the traffic on the key arteries in Bangkok is pretty bad during daytime and through to late evening. Practise just randomly saying these two words (assuming the traffic is bad when you are sitting in the cab) almost rhetorically to every single taxi driver you encounter over a month and note down their response and see if you can understand it and if not, either ask what they said or write it down phonetically and check in your books to see if you can work out what they said.

6. gâw ก็

Meaning – no literal meaning / also

Context – this is one of the most common words in Thai and can be one of the words that separates a foreign Thai speaker who sounds like a foreigner speaking Thai and one who sounds like a Thai speaker. 'Gâw' is fundamental to spoken Thai and is used in almost every other sentence in casual conversation. In spite of all that, it actually has no literal meaning and is simply used to provide a pause or rhythm to a sentence or soften the directness of the response or opinion. However, it can be used to mean '*also*'. Confused? Learn to use 'gâw' and you are guaranteed to impress any Thai person. Finally, note that 'gâw' is also used in conjunction with 'laéo' or 'dâai' and so on and these are listed separately.

Example:

Gâw...mâi róo sì.

ก็ไม่รู้สิ

Erm...I don't know.

This is an example of where 'gâw' is used as a pause or as English speakers would say "*well...*". As you will notice when you read through this book, 'gâw' is absolutely fundamental to normal everyday language and this form of 'gâw', where it lends cadence to the sentence is more important in Thai than '*well*' is in English.

Pǒm gâw mâi róo.

ผมก็ไม่รู้

I don't know either (I also don't know).

This is an example of where 'gâw' is used to mean '*also*' or '*too*'.

Mun gâw mâi kà-nàad nán.

มันก็ไม่ขนาดนั้น

It's not like that.

This is an example of 'gâw' being used to soften a rebuttal.

> **Tips / in my experience / insight:** *listen for 'gâw' in TV chat show interviews with actors or singers and you will hear it throughout, almost, in some cases, every third or fourth word and sometimes so fast that you may not catch the use of it if you are new to Thai. You often get 'káo gâw'…'laéo káo gâw'…' dtàe mun gâw' and so on with the 'gâw' said so quickly after the preceding word, it is barely a hard 'g' sound to the uninitiated ear. This indicates how important 'gâw' is in casual everyday speech; it does not add much, if anything, to the meaning but makes you sound natural and provides rhythm and cadence to your words.*
>
> *Note that I have spelt 'gâw' as a short sound, which it is in many instances but just like 'well…' in English, the length of the sound varies along a spectrum depending on the context. So, in some cases, where the speakers wants to pause a bit more, 'gâw' is a longer sound.*

7. krúp / kà ครับ คะ

Meaning – no literal meaning

Context – although all Thai learners will have learnt that 'krúp' / 'kà' is a word to signify respect and make a sentence more polite and more formal, it has other uses too that may not be so obvious. For example, often it can be used to simply say yes or agree (note that saying "châi" in some situations marks you as a complete beginner to Thai such as if someone asks you if you want to go, or if you like something, or if you want to use the tollway; instead, the correct response is to repeat the verb to mean yes or just say 'krúp' / 'kà').

Example:

Person A: Jàai dtang laéo châi mái? Person B: (Jàai laéo) Krúp.

คนแรก: จ่ายตังค์แล้วใช่ไหม คนที่สอง: ครับ

Person A: You've paid already, right? Person B: Yep.

'dtang' comes from the word for pence in Thai – 'sà-dtaang'.

Person A: Cheuhn nâng kà. Person B: Krúp.

คนแรก: เชิญนั่งคะ คนที่สอง: ครับ

Person A: Please take a seat. Person B: Ok / thanks.

'Cheuhn' is a fairly formal word that means *'invite'*. In this sentence, it sort of means *'I invite you to please take a seat'*. 'Chuan' is a less formal word for the verb to invite but cannot be used as *'please'* in the above sentence. Part of the reason is also that 'chuan' is slightly more active and persuasive than 'cheuhn', which is, as I said before, slightly more formal.

> **Tips / in my experience / insight:** *you obviously know this word and you may even know that you can use it to mean 'yes' or 'ok' but have you also heard the word "krúp-pŏm'? I'll leave you to find out if you haven't yet.*
>
> *If you pay attention you will hear phone conversations where the speaker is just saying "dâai krúp...krúp, krúp krúp... krúp-pŏm ... dâai krúp....kruúup....krúp...sa-wàt-dee krúp". Don't get wound up by this even if it might sound a bit annoying – it's actually no different to English where the person keeps saying "yeah, yep, sure, ok...no problem, ok, cheers".*

8. nai kà-nà têe ในขณะที่

Meaning – whereas / at the same time / while / all the while

Context – same as in English, this is a useful word when you want to describe something is happening or someone is doing something all the while while something else is happening as well. Alternatively, it can be used to simply compare two things and illustrate that they are very different. If you listen to Thai news you will hear this word a lot to transition from one news item to the next in the same way English newsreaders say "*meanwhile over in…*".

Example:

Pǒm lawng rian wâai náam maa lǎai kráng dtàe gâw yang wâai mâi bpen nai kà-nà têe kon èun rian sǎwng sǎam 'claat' (class) gâw bpen leuy.

ผมลองเรียนว่ายน้ำมาหลายครั้งแต่ก็ยังว่ายไม่เป็น ในขณะที่คนอื่น เรียนสองสามคลาสก็เป็นเลย

I have tried to learn to swim many times but still can't do it while others take a few classes and start swimming.

To 'lawng' something means to try and do something. So for example, you could say 'pǒm lawng bpai èeg taang neung', which would mean '*I tried going a different way*'.

'mâi bpen' and 'mâi dâai' are similar in meaning but there is a subtle and important difference. The former is usually used when talking about things that you do not have the skill or ability to do whereas the latter is more for things that you cannot do because of other reasons such as it is against the law or you were prevented from doing it.

But in some cases, the distinction has become blurred through usage, with the most apparent example being when people say "pôod tai mâi dâai" even though it should really be 'mâi bpen', which is more correct. In many other cases you cannot interchange the two and so the general rule applies such as if you want to say you cannot swim, you cannot say "wâai náam mâi dâai", which would only be appropriate if e.g. the conversation was about whether swimming is allowed in the sea, as opposed to your ability to swim.

Notice the use of 'bpen leuy' instead of repeating 'swim' – it basically means 'get it'.

> **Cultural insight / life in Thailand: Monarchy and politics**
>
> *One of the most awe inspiring moments you will have in Thailand is when you go to a cinema and stand for the King's anthem. The King of Thailand is revered among the Thai people and with good reason – the images you see from the King's life give you an idea of how much he has done personally for his country. You should never fail to stand for the King before your film and as I said, you will be rewarded with a great and moving song and images of the King.*
>
> *You may also be aware that you should not, under any circumstances, discuss the royal family in public if your comments are anything but wholly appreciative and respectful. You could get into serious trouble, which is not unreasonable since you are unlikely to have a good enough understanding of the monarchy or Thai history to be in a position to comment. Keep your opinions to yourself.*
>
> *And for the same reasons you should not discuss politics in Thailand under any circumstances. It is just as sensitive and much better avoided, especially since you probably don't understand it as well as you think you do so just don't offer opinions on politics.*

9. rîap róoi เรียบร้อย

Meaning – prim and proper / well mannered / finished / complete

Context – this is one of the most confusing words for those new to Thai. 'Rîap róoi' can be used in several ways but there is a loose common theme of being finished or presented properly. When describing people, a 'rîap róoi' girl is someone who is quite quiet and prim and proper and for men, a man who is well presented and possibly well organised in his lifestyle. As Thai (just like English) is a language where words can be used to indirectly criticise or poke fun or soften the delivery of an opinion i.e. deliver veiled insults, 'rîap róoi' can be used to suggest a girl who is a bit difficult to talk to and takes time to loosen up or a man who is a bit fussy and 'precious'. 'Rîap róoi' can also be used to state when something has been completed. How? Well, it is actually the same meaning in a sense – completed to a tidy and proper state or finished in good order. See?

Example:

Káo bpen pôo-yǐng kâwn kâang rîap róoi.

เขาเป็นผู้หญิงค่อนข้างเรียบร้อย

She is quite 'prim and proper'.

Person A: Sèt rěu yang? Person B: Rîap róoi.

คนแรก: เสร็จหรือยัง คนที่สอง: เรียบร้อย

Person A: Have you finished yet? Person B: Yep, all done (and completed in an orderly fashion).

The phrase 'sèt rěu yang?' literally means '*have you finished or not finished yet?*' and so can be quite an abrupt expression. Ensure you use the 'krúp' or 'kà' particle and a polite tone of voice to mitigate.

Wan née rao jà mee kàek maa yîam gâw leuy yàak hâi tóok kon chûai gan gèp ráan tam kwaam sà-àad láeo gâw gèp dtó gâo-êe hâi rîap róoi.

วันนี้เราจะมีแขกมาเยี่ยมก็เลยอยากให้ทุกคนช่วยกันเก็บร้าน ทำความสะอาด แล้วก็เก็บโต๊ะเก้าอี้ให้เรียบร้อย

Today we are going to have visitors so I would like you all to please help tidy up and clean the store and straighten out all the tables and chairs back to their place, thanks.

Notice the use of gâw leuy as a conjunction to link the first clause about having visitors and the second bit on telling the staff to tidy up.

10. laéo gun แล้วกัน 🇸 🇹🇭

Meaning – in that case / I'll settle for / no specific meaning

Context – this is another word used very often in spoken Thai and often serves just to soften the meaning or indicates the speaker will settle for an outcome. This is an example of the kind of word you need to be able to use to 'sound Thai'. You could say the sentence without laéo gun but adding it makes it a more humble, polite and conciliatory sentence rather than not using it, which often sounds abrupt in Thai, unlike in English. Note, in the examples below, I have written it as 'lá-gun', just to show the shortened spoken version.

Example:

Bpai 'Cen-tûn' (Central Department Store) mâi tun...ngún bpai ráan tăeo née lá-gun.

ไป 'เซ็นทัน' ไม่ทัน งั้นไปร้านแถวนี้ละกัน

Don't think we are going to make it to Central today so let's go to the local shop instead.

'mâi tun' is a useful expression to know; to 'tun' means to make it in time and there are several offshoots from this meaning such as 'dtaam mâi tun', which means '*cannot keep up*' (such as not being able to follow a movie plotline or the words to a song).

'tăeo' is used to indicate a locality or your surroundings so 'tăeo née' is used in the same way English speakers would say "*around here*".

Wài bpai èeg tee kraao nâa lá-gun.

ไว้ไปอีกทีคราวหน้าละกัน

Let's go some other time.

Notice the use of 'wài', which is short for 'ao wài', which means, '*let's leave it...*' and is used when making a suggestion to postpone something for later.

'èeg tee' means '*another time*' and so you can use it in many situations. For example, 'deuan nâa jà bpai èeg têe neung...' – '*I'm going again next month...*' and so on. Practise this phrase and test yourself on whether you can use it correctly and get a sensible response (demonstrating that the listener properly understood what you said).

Finally notice the use of 'kraao' to indicate time, not 'we-laa' so you cannot say 'we-laa nâa' for '*next time*'. But 'kraao' means something closer to how English speakers use '*chance*' so it's closer to '*the next chance we get*'.

> **Tips / in my experience / insight:** *laéo gun* is very, very common in Thai and therefore one of the perfect words to attempt to sound more Thai. One easy way is to say "*lawng doo laéo gun*", meaning "give it a go and see" at the end of a discussion any discussion where you would use the expression in English e.g. if you are discussing whether or not you should apply for a job that isn't exactly what you do but looks interesting. This is just one of a huge number of examples I am sure you can think of where you can use *laéo gun* because, as I said a the start, it is just a conciliatory word or a word to arrive at a resolution on a course of action.

11. jing jing (laéo) จริง ๆ แล้ว S

Meaning – Actually

Context – Just as in English, many sentences sound more natural when you add '*actually*' to the beginning. An alternative is just to shorten to 'jing jing'.

Example:

Jing jing laéo gâw yàak jà 'fit' gwàa née dtàe chuâng née mâi kôi mee we-laa, ngaan yôong mâak leuy.

จริงๆแล้วก็อยากจะฟิตกว่านี้ แต่ช่วงนี้ไม่ค่อยมีเวลา งานยุ่งมากเลย

Actually I would like to get fitter but I don't have a lot of time these days because work is so busy.

Practise using the word 'chuâng' and it will come in handy in many situations; it translates as a non-specific amount of time. You will hear 'chuâng' in just about any programe on TV when the presenters tell you at the end of the first half what is coming up after the commercial break, so you will hear 'chuâng nâa…'. Notice that in the sentence above 'chuâng née' means '*these days*' because, as mentioned already, it is not a defined period of time.

A rather interesting use of the word yôong is to just use it by itself. In this use, of course it can still mean just '*busy*' if someone asks whether you are busy but it can also mean '*none of your business!*' You will often hear women use yôong in this way. Basically it is a shorter version of 'yaa yôong…' how does it link to '*busy*'?...well, it is like we would say "*don't be a busybody/don't interfere*". See? Quite interesting.

12. jà bàwk hâi จะบอกให้

Meaning – I can tell you (that for sure) / I'm telling you

Context – this is one of the words Thai people use to state a firm opinion such as when you have achieved something that others would not believe you could. Alternatively, it is often used when you want to state some facts or opinions that are quite amazing or hard to believe. It can be slightly girly but only slightly and is still fine for men to use.

Example:

Chán mâi mee wan ngôh bpai kóp pêe chaai teuh bpen faen ràwk ná jà bàwk hâi.

ฉันไม่มีวันโง่ไปคบพี่ชายเธอเป็นแฟนหรอกนะ จะบอกให้

"There's no way I'm going to get involved with (or more precisely, "date") your brother, I'm telling you.

> **Tips / in my experience / insight:** *by its very nature, this word is a bit self-righteous and dramatic. So it is again one of those words where a foreigner saying it with those tones will be funny (in a good way). Often this type of expression can break the ice and the cultural barrier and help to bring you closer to Thai people. The example above however is a much more stronger sentiment where 'jà bàwk hâi' is used to intensify the sentence.*

13. sêung ซึ่ง

Meaning – which

Context – this is quite a tricky word to get used to in Thai. Although it means '*which*', the way it is used sometimes seems subtly different to English and takes some practice. In Thai, it can be used to make a statement and then use 'sêung' to qualify that statement or provide more colour. This is one of the words that will separate you from the average Thai speaker…if you can use it correctly of course.

Example:

Dǐao née dèk châwp lên pûak 'Fáde-bóok' (Facebook), 'Tá-wít dtêuh' (Twitter), Instagram, a-rai yàng née-a, sêung, nai kwaam hěn pǒm, pǒm wâa mâi mee bprà-yòht; kuan jà hâi káo àwk bpai lên gee-laa mâak gwàa.

เดี๋ยวนี้เด็กชอบเล่นพวกเฟสบุ๊ค ทวิตเตอร์ อินสตาแกรมอะไรอย่างนี้ ซึ่งในความเห็นผม ผมว่าไม่มีประโยชน์ ควรจะให้เขาออกไปเล่นกีฬามากกว่า

These days kids spend time on the Internet and Facebook and so on, which, in my opinion, is a waste of time; they should get out and play sports.

Dtua née kǎai dee sêung bpen dtua têe chún lêuak eng.

ตัวนี้ขายดีซึ่งเป็นตัวที่ฉันเลือกเอง

This one (e.g. item of clothing) is selling well and happens to be one that I personally chose.

Sîn bpee née yàak bpai tîao Yêe-bpòon. Káo bàwk wâa Yêe-bpòon bpen bprà-têt têe sŭay láeo gâw mee wát-tá-ná-tam têe nâa sŏn jai lăai yàang sêung, pŏm gâw hĕn dûai.

สิ้นปีนี้อยากไปเที่ยวญี่ปุ่น เขาบอกว่าญี่ปุ่นเป็นประเทศที่สวยแล้วก็มีวัฒนธรรมที่น่าสนใจหลายอย่าง ซึ่งผมก็เห็นด้วย

I want to go to Japan at the end of this year. They say it is a beautiful country and has lots of interesting culture, something which I think is true.

Notice the fact that usually (but certainly not always), where there is a time context, the time word - Sîn bpee – comes at the start of the sentence to set the context. This is more important in Thai where verbs do not conjugate and rely on the time context in many cases to decide the tense of the action.

Also notice the phrase 'Káo bàwk wâa', which translates directly into English. This is a commonly used expression when people are talking about things they have heard somewhere or have some vague knowledge of in exactly the same way as in English speech.

14. yang dee ยังดี S

Meaning – still good / ok

Context – 'yang dee' is probably more common in Thai than the literal translation is in English. It is used when something has not quite worked out to the expected level but the end result is still not too bad.

Example:

(Assume conversation about going to a condo opening).
Gâw yang dee, yàng nóoi rao gâw dâi maa doo condo mài. Těung wan née 'bpro-mo-chún' jà mòt bpai láeo dtàe dǐao deuan nâa gâw mee èeg. Wái kôi maa mài dtawn nán gâw dâai.

ก็ยังดี อย่างน้อยเราก็ได้มาดูคอนโดใหม่ ถึงวันนี้โปรโมชั่นจะหมดไปแล้ว แต่เดี๋ยวเดือนหน้าก็มีอีก ไว้ค่อยมาใหม่ตอนนั้นก็ได้

Doesn't matter (literally, "it's still good"), at least we got to take a look at a new condo. Even though we missed out on the promotion today, there will be another one next month so we can just go then.

'yàng nóoi', meaning '*at least*' is a useful phrase and easy to practise – if you hear someone give a negative opinion or state a less than ideal state of affairs, you can deliberately take the opposite view and see if you can create a sentence with 'yàng nóoi'.

Also, have you noticed the use of 'dâi maa doo...'? The addition of the 'dâi' in front of the verb is equivalent to '*we got to do...*' in English. Another good type of expression to practise.

'dǐao' and 'gâw dâai' are explained elsewhere so for now, I will only say that they are so common in everyday speech that it is well worth trying to notice every conversation (on TV or in real life) where these words are spoken and see if you can get a feel for when to use them and how. These types of words are the difference between someone who sounds natural in Thai and someone who is more rigid, staccato or simply someone who the listener is acutely aware is a learner of Thai and therefore thinks is not able to have a real conversation with. You will only be able to have meaningful conversations with Thai people when you make the effort to notice how Thai people speak Thai and copy those key connecting and cadence enhancing words, not the rote learnt formal phrases, which mark you as a beginner.

> **Cultural insight / life in Thailand: Don't out-Thai Thais**
>
> *When you are new to Thailand or if you are on holiday, it is often intoxicating to learn a new exotic culture and this can be extremely rewarding and therefore highly recommended. The more you understand the culture and the environment, the more you can appreciate the people. BUT, don't try to be more Thai than Thai people. Don't forget who you are and where you come from.*
>
> *You do not need to use the non air-conditioned buses because you think this is what Thai people do and you do not need to eat by the side of the road every day and you do not need to like sôm-dtam necessarily (if you do, great). You can respect Thai people and their choices and equally, you are perfectly entitled to make yours. And, guess what, just because you see people eating for 30 baht doesn't mean that represents all Thai people.*
>
> *In line with this, don't initiate a wâi to shop staff or younger people or taxi drivers etc. It is not really the right thing to do and makes the recipient feel a little awkward and is not something that a Thai person would do. Generally speaking, the person with seniority, whether by age or social or situational status wâis the other first, so customers are shown respect by getting wâi'd first by staff. A polite mini-head bow or nod is fine; if you get wâi'd, definitely wâi back.*

15. lĕua wái เหลือไว้

Meaning – left over / leave it there for...

Context – '<u>wái</u>' can be used in this way to indicate that the verb in question is something to be done for a continuous period of time.

Example:

Lĕua <u>wái</u> <u>hâi</u> <u>chún</u> bâang <u>ná</u>! <u>Chún</u> <u>gin</u> <u>mâi</u> <u>reo</u> mĕuan teuh.

เหลือไว้ให้ฉันกินบ้างนะ ฉันกินไม่เร็วเหมือนเธอ

Leave some for me! I don't eat as quickly as you.

Near the end of the book I discuss another meaning of '<u>hâi</u>' but in this case above, it is fairly straightforward – it means '*for*' and could have been substituted with '<u>pêua</u>' or '<u>sămrùp</u>', which both mean '*for*' too.

'<u>ao</u> <u>bpai</u>' and '<u>ao</u> maa' are words that I still have a little trouble with even today after over ten years of speaking Thai. Perhaps the reason is that these words are single words in English – '*take*' and '*bring*'.

To make matters worse, in English, if you are speaking to someone about going somewhere where that other person is present already, you would use '*come*', not '*go*' e.g. "*when do you want me to come over?*"

In Thai, you would still use '<u>bpai</u>' because the only thing that is relevant is the fact that you are going from where you are located to somewhere else, not the fact that the person you are talking to is already at that place and so you are **coming** to him / her.

I also sometimes get confused between 'bpai sòng' (send (when you physically go somewhere to do so)) or send someone off e.g. to the train station), 'sòng bpai' (you send outbound), 'maa sòng' (when somebody will physically deliver something to you) and 'sòng maa' (the sender sends to you - inbound) so worth learning these properly so that you are clear.

> **Cultural insight / life in Thailand: You are being assessed!**
>
> *This sounds crazy, right? Do you really need to be reminded that you are a foreigner and not Thai? That all eyes are on you. Well, actually, as a matter of fact, yes, you do.*
>
> *It can be easy to not even be aware of these things when you are new to Thailand (for work or residence, not a holiday) because you do not yet understand your environment and you do not even realize the fact that all eyes are on you. The other time you can become complacent and forget is when you have become good at Thai and comfortable with life in Thailand.*
>
> *You are pretty much being watched and assessed by your colleagues and neighbours. And they all talk! About you! Yes, I am presenting this in a sensational, paranoid way but there is an underlying truth to it and actually there is nothing malicious about all this talk about you...at least, not initially. The problem usually is that if you are a foreigner, you are already in the spotlight so every move and word of yours is noted and also that you are not used to behaving as inconspicuously as Thai people. You may talk louder, be used to talking about your weekend activities, be open about your dating etc. Whether you care if people talk is up to you.*

16. kâwn kâang (têe jà) ค่อนข้าง

Meaning – pretty much / quite a bit

Context – this word is often used when you want to characterize something or someone. It serves to soften your opinion slightly by not saying something or someone is fully as per your opinion but rather, '*seems like*' or is '*pretty much*' or similar. In fact, in many cases, when Thai people use 'kâwn kâang', they actually do think the subject of their opinion is bad or lazy or clever or whatever the opinion may be but they use the word to be diplomatic in public.

Example:

Tà-nǒn sên nân kâwn kâang an-dtà-raai – rót wîng reo mâak dtawn glaang keun laéo gâw gèuhd où-bà-dtì-hèd bòi.

ถนนเส้นนั้นค่อนข้างอันตราย รถวิ่งเร็วมากตอนกลางคืน แล้วก็เกิดอุบัติเหตุบ่อย

That road is quite dangerous. The cars drive really fast at night and there are often accidents.

Notice the use of the classifier 'sên' – it is well worth learning the main classifiers in Thai such as 'lǎng' for houses or 'dtua' for items of clothes for example. Imagine if someone said "can you buy 2 breads" in English!

Next, notice the use of 'wîng' – mostly known as the verb to run – to describe cars being driven. This is very, very common in Thai so listen out for it.

Dtua née kâwn kâang tòok dtàe yang deuhn doo mâi mòt leuy…ao yàng née, bpai doo ráan èun gàwn, tâa mâi jeuh dtua năi tòok jai gwàa, kôi glàp maa séu dtua née gâw laéo gun.

ตัวนี้ค่อนข้างถูกแต่ยังเดินดูไม่หมดเลย เอาอย่างนี้ ไปดูร้านอื่นก่อน ถ้าไม่เจอตัวไหนถูกใจกว่าค่อยกลับมาซื้อตัวนี้ก็แล้วกัน

This one (e.g. a table from Ikea) is quite a good price but there are lots of other stores…tell you what, why don't we go and check out a few other shops and if we don't see anything we like, we can come back and get this one.

'ao yàng ngée' is a phrase I discuss in the next book but for now, as you can see, it is a very useful expression to link sentences seamlessly. Again, this is the kind of expression that will give you credibility as a Thai speaker.

tòok jai is quite a common expression and will be relevant in many situations in your daily life so learn to use it. Sometimes it is better than using the same old châwp all the time. Literally, it means to touch your heart – the verb tòok means to touch.

As you will have noticed in many of the sentences so far and later in this book, there are hardly any pronouns. This is quite unnatural to an English speaker, who, like myself, always feels the need to say "I" even if it is obvious who you are referring to. One point to emphasise is that if you do retain a few unnecessary pronouns in your speech, by no means is that wrong and over time you will naturally omit more. So don't stress about pronouns.

17. bpò-kà-dtì ปกติ

Meaning – normally

Context – same as in English

Example:

Bpò-kà-dtì châwp bpai àwk gam lang gaai dtawn cháao. Mun tam hâi róo sèuk sót-chêun laéo gâw grà-bprêe-grà-bprào táng wan; dee gwàa bpai àwk dtawn yen lăng lêuhk ngaan láeo sòot-táai gâw mâi dâi bpai práw nèuay laéo.

ปกติชอบไปออกกำลังกายตอนเช้า มันทำให้รู้สึกสดชื่นแล้วก็กระปรี้กระเปร่าทั้งวัน ดีกว่าไปออกตอนเย็นหลังเลิกงาน แล้วสุดท้ายก็ไม่ได้ไปเพราะเหนื่อยแล้ว

Normally I work out in the morning. It makes you feel fresh and gives you energy for the rest of the day. It's better than leaving it until the evening after work and then you end up not going because you're too tired.

Wan née hĕn kon bon rót fai fáa kon neung têe tam dtua mâi kôi bpò-kà-dtì. Tóok kon mawng káo dtàe káo gâw mâi sŏn jai.

วันนี้เห็นคนบนรถไฟฟ้าคนนึงทำตัวไม่ค่อยปกติ ทุกคนมองเขาแต่เขาก็ไม่สนใจ

Today I saw a guy acting strangely on the skytrain. Everyone was staring at him but he didn't care.

18. nêe ngai นี่ไง

Meaning – here it is

Context – can be slightly girly and is more commonly used by women but this is still an acceptable word for men to use. It is suitable for any situation where you have come upon the thing you were just talking about or are searching for in your room or similar. As you will notice with other uses of 'ngai', it often serves to make the preceding word a little more direct and this case is the same – 'nêe' by itself means '*here*' and the 'ngai' makes it more of an exclamation.

Example:

Person A: Hăa toh-rá-sàp maa bpen chûa mohng láeo yang mâi jeuh leuy, seng! Person B: Yòo nêe ngai.

คนแรก: หาโทรศัพท์มาเป็นชั่วโมงแล้วยังไม่เจอเลย เซ็ง คนที่สอง: อยู่นี่ไง

Person A: Aargh, I'm sick of it…I've been looking for my mobile for hours now and still can't find it. Person B: Here it is. (As compared to 'It's here' without 'ngai')

Notice the way of saying 'bpen chûa mohng', which equates to '*for hours*'; not necessarily that the phone was being searched for one hour exactly so like the English that it '*feels like ages*'.

'seng' is a stronger version of 'bèua' and so worth being a bit careful when and with whom it is used.

Finally, notice the omission of 'mun' in the reply – where it is obvious or where the inclusion of the pronoun does not add any meaning to the sentence, it can and usually is omitted.

19. krai jà bpai róo ใครจะไปรู้

Meaning – who would know / how am I supposed to know

Context – used when an outcome has occurred based on a reason or factors that you had no way of knowing. Notice that you do not say 'krai jà róo', which is technically correct but the addition of 'bpai' makes the sentiment more powerful, just as in English you could say "*how would I go and know*" or "*how was I supposed to know*".

Example:

Oòt-sàa dtàeng dtua dee jà bpai kui gùp 'sale' kǎai condo; krai jà bpai róo wâa káo bpìd wan jan. Dǐao wái kôi bpai èeg tee lǎng leûhk ngaan prôong nêe gâw laéo gun.

อุตส่าห์แต่งตัวดีจะไปคุยกับเซลล์ขายคอนโด ใครจะไปรู้ว่าเขาปิดวันจันทร์ เดี๋ยวไว้ค่อยไปอีกทีหลังเลิกงานพรุ่งนี้ก็แล้วกัน

I got all dressed up to go and meet (literally "speak to") the condo sales lady; how was I supposed to know that they are closed on Mondays. In that case, I'll go again after work tomorrow.

'Oòt-sàa' is quite a useful word to know for any situation where you want to say you went to the effort of doing something or the event that you have been anticipating and preparing for is not going ahead and so on.

'dtàeng' is a verb used for several meanings e.g. 'dtàeng rót' means to customise your car and 'dtàeng ngaan' means to marry; a literal translation of 'dtàeng' is '*decorate*'.

Notice that I could have inserted 'pêua têe jà' between 'dtàeng dtua dee' and 'jà bpai kui' if I had wanted in order to be more correct and verbose.

I have already used 'dǐao' in previous example sentences and again here so hopefully you should be getting a good idea of how it is used in Thai.

'lǎng leûhk ngaan' is bound to be a useful expression for most people so worth practising the pronunciation and some example sentences. For example, imagine your partner suggests going to watch a movie and you want to suggest going after work or how about suggesting to your colleagues to go for a meal / drink after work. You should find that just this one short phrase could lead to you learning tens or maybe even hundreds of new words and word combinations and variations once you explore each strand of conversation that could originate from this phrase and memorise and learn all the rest of the words in these conversations.

> **Tips / in my experience / insight:** *just as in English, the phrase 'krai jà bpai róo' is a bit melodramatic so it is not really suitable for the average situation but one interesting way to use it is to deliberately use it to sound deliberately over the top and despairing, which can be quite funny to a native speaker when it is a foreigner who is skilled enough in Thai to understand subtleties like this. And in fact, the same goes for most of the 'feminine' or other melodramatic ways of expression – you can use these to your advantage to be more humourous and bond with local speakers.*

20. yók dtua yàang (chên) ยกตัวอย่าง

Meaning – I'll give you an example / for example

Context – the word 'yók' literally means 'to raise' and so you can see how it is relevant: 'let me raise an example' in literal terms. Notice 'chên' is often added / substituted.

Example:

Têe meuang tai, gaan bo-rí-gaan koon-ná-pâap dee mâak tîap gùp bprà-têt eun eun. Yók dtua yàang, mêua waan gàwn pǒm bpai séu wâen dtaa; pá-nák-ngaan kǎai pôod-jaa sù-pâap láeo gâw doo lae dee mâak. Tǎam a-rai náwng káo gâw yin dee dtàwb mòt laéo gâw chûai lêuak yàang gùp bpen pêuan.

Gaan têe pá-nák-ngaan kǎai kǎwng doo lae ao jai lôok-káa tam hâi gaan bpai 'cháwp-bpîng' bpen sing têe rao châwp tam we-laa yòo meuang tai kà-nà têe bprà-têt èun mee ráan yài gwàa dee gwàa dtàe rao gláp mâi róo-sèuk sà-nòok měuan gùp we-laa 'cháwp-bpîng' nai meuang tai. Sêung nâa jà bpen hèd-pǒn neung têe mee kon dtàang châat maa 'cháwp-bpîng' têe Groong-Têp yéuh mâak – práw nâwk jàak sǐn-káa jà raa-kaa tòok láeo gaan bo-rí-gaan gâw dee mâak dûai.

ที่เมืองไทยการบริการคุณภาพดีมากเทียบกับประเทศอื่นๆ ยกตัวอย่าง เมื่อวานก่อนผมไปซื้อแว่นตา พนักงานขายพูดจาสุภาพแล้วก็ดูแลดีมาก ถามอะไรน้องเขาก็ยินดีตอบหมด แล้วก็ช่วยเลือกอย่างกับเป็นเพื่อน

การที่พนักงานขายของดูแลเอาใจใส่ลูกค้าทำให้การ

ไป "ช้อปปิ้ง" เป็นสิ่งที่เราชอบทำเวลาอยู่เมืองไทย ขณะที่ประเทศอื่นมีร้านใหญ่กว่าดีกว่าแต่เรากลับไม่รู้สึกสนุกเหมือนกับเวลา "ช้อปปิ้ง" ในเมืองไทย

Service in Thailand is really good compared to some other countries. For example, the other day I was buying some spectacles and the sales girl was so polite and took care of me really well. She was happy to answer all my questions and helped me choose the right one almost as if she was my friend.

The way that staff look after you and go out of their way to make the customer happy is what makes shopping so enjoyable in Thailand whereas in other countries, even if there are bigger and better stores, shopping doesn't quite give the same feeling. That's probably the reason so many foreigners go to Bangkok for shopping – apart from the low prices, the service is also really good.

Learn your 'bo-rí…' words: 'bo-rí -gaan' – 'service', 'bo-rí-wen' – 'area' or 'region', 'bo-rí-jàak' – 'donate', 'bo-rí-sòot' – 'pure' or 'virgin', 'bo-rí-hăan' – 'manage' and so on.

Another useful expression is 'nâa jà bpen', which is one of many expressions using 'nâa' that is a key feature of Thai expression but does not exist in English. 'nâa lawng' means 'worth trying' and 'nâa gliat' means 'ugly' or 'disgusting' and comes from the literal translation 'worthy of being hated'. As well as these expressions where 'nâa' means worthy of… whatever the verb is, it is also used to mean 'likely to', as in the expression 'nâa jà bpen' or 'nâa jà dâai', which means 'will probably get' or 'have a good chance of getting' and so on. Learn to use 'nâa' and you will have a multitude of new ways of expressing yourself from this small simple word.

21. dang nán / práw-chà-nán ดังนั้น / เพราะฉะนั้น

Meaning – therefore

Context – both words are relatively formal but can still be used in everyday conversation. In my own experience, I have heard 'dang nán' less in everyday situations compared to 'práw-chà-nán'. 'Dang nán' is used in more semi-formal situations such as, for example, by TV presenters on factual or current affairs programmes.

Example:

Dǐao née gaan pôod paa-sǎa ang-grìt sǎm-kan mâak yîng kêun gwàa sà-mǎi gàwn èeg. Dang nán rao leuy hěn kon tai rian paa-sǎa ang-grìt rěu tam-ngaan dtàang bprà-têt yéuh sêung pǒm mawng wâa bpen rêuang têe dee.

เดี๋ยวนี้การพูดภาษาอังกฤษสำคัญมากยิ่งขึ้นกว่าสมัยก่อนอีก ดังนั้นเราเลยเห็นคนไทยเรียนภาษาอังกฤษหรือทำงานต่างประเทศเยอะ ซึ่งผมมองว่าเป็นเรื่องที่ดี

The ability to speak English is even more important these days compared to before (the old days). That's why you see more and more Thai people studying English or working abroad, which is a good thing in my opinion.

'Dǐao née' is a good alternative to 'chûang née'.

Notice the use of 'yîng', which means '*even more*' and practise it.

Notice you cannot use 'deuhm' to refer to '*before*' because it is a bit more specific and means the state of affairs previously so, for example, 'nóoi gwàa deuhm' means '*less than before*' and 'we-laa deuhm' means '*the same time (as the previous occasion)*'.

22. (sêung) nai kwaam bpen jing ในความเป็นจริง

Meaning – in reality

Context – very similar to 'jing jing laéo' but I have listed this separately because there is enough subtle difference between the two, whether in Thai or English. Also, it allows another chance to show the use of 'sêung', which is often used to precede this word.

Example:

Ráan née mâi kôi bpen têe róo jàk nai mòo kon dtàang châat práw mâi mâi mee 'mae-noo' (menu) paa-săa ang-grìt sêung, nai kwaam bpen jing, mâi nâa jà bpen bpan-hăa a-rai práw pá-nák ngaan 'sèrf' (serve) tóok kon pôod paa-săa ang-grìt bpen.

ร้านนี้ไม่ค่อยเป็นที่รู้จักในหมู่คนต่างชาติ เพราะไม่มีเมนูภาษาอังกฤษ ซึ่งในความเป็นจริงก็ไม่น่าจะเป็นปัญหาอะไร เพราะพนักงานเสิร์ฟทุกคนพูดภาษาอังกฤษเป็น

This restaurant is not that well known because they do not have English menus but in reality it isn't an issue because their staff all speak English.

You must have noticed many times already but just in case not, remember verbs come at the end of the sentence or clause in Thai so you don't say "...pôod bpen paa-săa ang-grìt" or "...dâi pôod paa-săa ang-grìt", where the former means to say it in English, not the ability to speak English and the latter would mean '*...got (the chance) to speak English*'. (As mentioned at the start of the book, 'dâi' changes to a shorter sound when it precedes the verb to retain the rhythm and momentum of that cluster of words, which is obviously a huge factor in a tonal language).

23. sùan... ส่วน...

Meaning – on his / her part / as for him / her

Context – 'sùan' literally translated means '*part*'. In this context, 'sùan' is used to when you want to relate a story or incident where there are two protagonists – you state what you want to say about the first person and then say 'sùan...', meaning '*on his part...*' or '*as for*' to link to the comparison of the second person's case.

Example:

Wan née bpai săwn dèk maa săwng kon. Kon râek kâo jai cháa nòi, dtâwng a-tí-baai lăai kráng, sùan èeg kon neung, pôod gèng mâak mĕuan kon ang-grìt leuy.

วันนี้ไปสอนเด็กมาสองคน คนแรกเข้าใจช้าหน่อย ต้องอธิบายหลายครั้ง ส่วนอีกคนหนึ่งพูดเก่งมาก เหมือนคนอังกฤษเลย

Today I went to teach two kids; the first was a little slow and I had to explain the same thing several times over, whereas (alternatively, "As for") the other kid was so smart and could speak just like a native English speaker!

Did you notice the classifier for people – 'dèk săwng kon'? Learn classifiers and prevent yourself from making major faux pas like saying "rong-rian rao mee yee-sìp kroo"!

Náwng chaai (kǎwng) <u>pǒm</u> <u>bpen</u> <u>tá</u>-naai-kwaam, sùan pêe-sǎao <u>pêung</u> laa-àwk jàak ngaan maa yòo bâan <u>práw</u> wâa <u>gam</u> <u>lang</u> <u>jà</u> mee lôok.

น้องชาย (ของ) ผมเป็นทนายความ ส่วนพี่สาวเพิ่งลาออกจากงานมาอยู่บ้านเพราะว่ากำลังจะมีลูก

My brother is a lawyer and my sister has left her job so that she can stay at home because she is going to have a baby soon.

Here is another feature of Thai — where it does not destroy the rhythm of the sentence too much or simply where you want to be succinct, you can omit the 'kǎwng' when talking in the possessive case.

Also, as mentioned before, I could have omitted the pronoun too, reducing the whole thing to 'Náwng chaai <u>bpen</u>...'.

'<u>pêung</u>' is useful for simple responses such as when someone asks when you came home, you can simply say '<u>pêung</u> maa' or '<u>pêung</u> (maa) <u>těung</u>' for '*just arrived*' or '<u>pêung</u> <u>kâo</u> <u>jai</u>', which means '*I just got it*'.

24. baang tee บางที

Meaning – perhaps / maybe / sometimes

Context – this is quite useful to tone down your opinions or statements to be more modest or humble or subtle. It can be used to precede opinions to adjust them from "*I think…*" to "*Well, I suppose…*" and so one of the words that make you sound Thai if used properly. It is often paired with 'aàd-jà' – '*maybe*'.

Example:

Baang tee káo aàd-jà mâi dâi dtâng jai tam gâw dâai.

บางทีเขาอาจจะไม่ได้ตั้งใจทำก็ได้

He probably didn't mean to do it.

Baang tee tâa mee sa-tăa-nee rót fai fáa mâak gwàa née, bprà-chaa-chon àad jà mâi dtâwng deuhn taang bpai năi maa năi dooy chái rót-yon bpen làk.

บางทีถ้ามีสถานีรถไฟฟ้ามากกว่านี้ ประชาชนอาจจะไม่ต้องเดินทางไปไหนมาไหนโดยใช้รถยนต์เป็นหลัก

Perhaps if there were more skytrain stations, people would not use their car to go everywhere.

'rót yon' is the full word for '*car*'; 'rót' by itself, is the generic word for cars, buses, vans, coaches, lorries, trains but when it is obvious you are talking about cars, you can use just 'rót'.

25. tâa mâi kíd a-rai mâak ถ้าไม่คิดอะไรมาก

Meaning – if you are not that fussy / if you don't mind

Context – translated literally, this means *'if you don't think too much'* and is used in any situation where you want to suggest something which may not be exactly what the other person may need or where your suggestion has some minor drawbacks but still may be acceptable.

Example:

Gâw...tâa mâi kíd a-rai mâak...gâw leûak 'yoo-nìt' (unit) têe chán jèd gâw dâai. 'Wiw' (view) aàd-jà mâi kôi sǔay dtàe dtawn née gam-lang mee 'bpro-moh-chûn' (promotion) raa-kaa kâwn-kâang tòok sǎm-rùp hâwng kà-nàad tâo née.

ก็ถ้าไม่คิดอะไรมากก็เลือกยูนิตที่ชั้น 7 ก็ได้ อาจจะวิวไม่ค่อยสวยแต่ตอนนี้กำลังมีโปรโมชั่น ราคาค่อนข้างถูกสำหรับห้องขนาดเท่านี้

Well if you are not too bothered about the view, maybe you should go for the unit on the 7th floor. They have a promotion on now and the price is quite cheap for a unit of this size.

Did you notice the phrase 'gam-lang mee'? That is how you say something is ongoing as you speak. And if you wanted to say that something is about to happen or start, you can add 'jà' before 'mee'.

Learn your 'tâo' words and find opportunities to use them and maybe even use more than one in sentence – 'tâo rai', 'tâo nán', 'tâo têe', 'tâo gun'.

26. laéo gâw แล้วก็

Meaning – and then/and

Context – this is a very, very common word, as are all uses of '<u>gâw</u>' and is a very useful word in many situations where one thing follows the other or something happens after a certain amount of time.

Example:

<u>Kùp</u> <u>bpai</u> rêuay rêuay èeg sǎwng róoi 'met' (metres) laéo <u>jà</u> <u>hěn</u> bpâai kǎwng condo dâan sáai.

ขับไปเรื่อยๆ อีกสองร้อย'เมตร' แล้วจะเห็นป้ายของคอนโดด้านซ้าย

Keep going for another 200 metres and you will see a sign for the condo on the left hand side.

Admittedly I did not use laéo <u>gâw</u> above – the <u>gâw</u> is not needed.

Notice the use of '<u>rêuay rêuay</u>', which is explained in its own right later in this book, to mean '*continuously*'.

Learn to use '<u>dâan</u>' and '<u>fàng</u>' and '<u>kâang</u>' to mean '*(left/right hand) side*' (of a road, for example).

<u>Wan</u> née <u>jà</u> <u>bpai</u> <u>sà</u> <u>pǒm</u> têe ráan laéo <u>gâw</u> <u>jà</u> <u>bpai</u> s<u>éu</u> kǎwng <u>kâo</u> bâan dtàw.

วันนี้จะไปสระผมที่ร้าน แล้วก็จะไปซื้อของเข้าบ้านต่อ

I am going to the hair salon to wash my hair and then I am going to get a few groceries afterward.

27. Sŏm-móod wâa สมมติว่า

Meaning – assume / let's say… / suppose

Context – a word that often comes up in conversation because you are often in the situation where you want to ask what someone would do in a particular set of circumstances in order to know what you should do yourself.
Example:

Sŏm-móod wâa rao bpai gun săam kon, jà bpai wan năi dee?

สมมติว่าเราไปกันสามคน จะไปวันไหนดี

Let's just say it's the three of us going…which day is good?

Learn to use 'dee' in the way above as an alternative to the more slightly more formal *'what day should we go?'* And then extend to other expressions that use 'dee' such as 'tam yang ngai dee?' – *'what should I do?'* and so on.

Sŏm-móod pŏm jà hăa ngaan nai meuang tai, kuan jà tam yang ngai bâang?

สมมติผมจะหางานในเมืองไทยควรจะทำยังไงบ้าง

If I was to look for a job in Thailand where should I start / what should I do?

I discuss 'bâang' in the next book but here is an example. Listen out for it.

28. gâw dâai ก็ได้ S

Meaning – ok / sure / no problem / whatever / maybe

Context – this is one of the most common words in Thai and can be used in an absolute multitude of different situations. As with 'laéo gâw' and just 'gâw' by itself, these words are so frequently used you cannot possibly miss them in just about any situation where Thai is being spoken informally. Formal Thai does not use 'gâw' or derivatives of this word very much but when are you ever going to speak formally anyway? Again, 'gâw daai' is one of the best words to learn to use naturally in order to sound Thai and really impress your friends or other local acquaintances. Literally, it means 'well...can'. And it can also be used to be make open minded and non-judgemental statements (example below) – one of several ways of how it can be used as a softener.

Example:

Person A: Bpai gin kâao ráan deuhm mái? Kêe gìat deuhn glai, mêuay kǎa. Person B: Gâw dâai.

คนแรก: ไปกินข้าวร้านเดิมไหม ขี้เกียจเดินไกล เมื่อยขา คนที่สอง: ก็ได้

Person A: Shall we go to eat at the same place as last time? Don't want to walk too far, my feet are aching. Person B: Sure.

Again, as per earlier in the book, notice the use of 'deuhm' – very useful because in Thai it saves a longer explanation about '*the place you went to last time*' by capturing it in one word.

'Kêe giat' means '*lazy*' and can be used to mean '*I can't be bothered*' as in the example sentence above. You can use this word to say quite a funny expression that should make your Thai friends laugh with surprise: try saying "kêe giat sǎn lǎng yaao" when someone is being lazy or reluctant to do something. It's a put-down so say it in a good-natured, melodramatic, over-the-top way and it will be funny and nobody will take any offence. Ask your friends to explain the expression to you afterward.

Káo aàd-jà mâi dâi dtâng-jai gâw dâai.

เขาอาจจะไม่ได้ตั้งใจก็ได้

Well it is possible that / maybe he didn't mean to do it.

> **Tips / in my experience / insight:** *if you are or you want to be the easy-going, go-with-the-flow kind of person that tends to survive longer in Thailand, use '<u>gâw</u> dâai' now and then. When people suggest something, repeat the suggestion and say '<u>gâw</u> dâai' or just '<u>gâw</u> dâai' and let the Thai person or group you are with make the decision. If you are new to Thailand, this is often the best option anyway. Of course if you say '<u>gâw</u> dâai' to absolutely everything, people will wonder what's wrong with you!*

29. săa-mâad...dâai สามารถ...ได้

Meaning – able to / can

Context – this is another word for '*can*' but is used in situations where you want to say "*you are able to*" or "*it is possible to*" if you were to say it formally. This is one word that, if you can use it properly, will earn you a lot of respect, especially if you understand when to use 'săa-mâad' and when to use 'dâai'.

Example:

Taang née gâw săa-mâad bpai dâai mĕuan gun. Aàd-jà glai gwàa níd nòi dtàe rót mâi dtìd.

ทางนี้ก็สามารถไปได้เหมือนกัน อาจจะไกลกว่านิดหน่อยแต่รถไม่ติด

You can go this way as well. It might be a little farther but less jammed.

'Glai': one of the trickiest things in Thai is ensuring you do say '*far*' and not '*near*' when you mean '*far*'. Sounds crazy, right? When you are talking at full speed, it can be a challenge to make sure you get the tone right, which is the only thing that differentiates '*near*' and '*far*'! You could be forgiven for thinking it quite sadistic that directly opposite meanings sound almost exactly the same to an English ear but it's a good reminder that Thai is a tonal language and so pronunciation is paramount. Practise and you will be fine.

Jòp bpà-rin-yaa-dtree laéo rao sǎa-mâad tam ngaan a-rai dâai dtâng lǎai yàang.

จบปริญญาตรีแล้วเราสามารถทำงานอะไรได้ตั้งหลายอย่าง

After you graduate you have a choice of lots of different jobs.

I will discuss 'rao' (it does not exactly mean '*we*' here) and other pronouns that you may not be familiar with in the next book.

Also, notice that the words in between 'sǎa-mâad' and 'dâai' can vary in length – they do not have to be just one verb. Basically the 'sǎa-mâad' and the 'dâai' are book-ends that couch your intended explanation of the action within them. So, you could even have 'sǎa-mâad bpèuht ban-chee láeo fàak ngeuhn wan diao gun dâai – '*you can open an account and deposit money into the account on the same day*'.

Listen out for these kinds of phrases, which you will encounter in semi-formal situations such as talking with a customer services officer at a bank, as in this example above.

> **Tips / in my experience / insight:** *watch Thai TV or listen to Thai radio (e.g. when you are in a cab) for this word as it is a slightly more formal word than is necessary to be used in casual conversation. You will hear many cases of the TV presenter telling you of things you are able to do e.g. that you are able to go to a specified website for further information, or, on the radio, the live traffic update telling drivers that they can use this or that alternative route. If you listen carefully you may hear the pronoun 'tûn' to refer to you, the listener, which I discuss in the next book.*

30. ao bpen wâa เอาเป็นว่า S

Meaning – how about this...? / let's settle for...

Context – used mainly when negotiating or trying to reach an agreement on a course of action and so suggest an approach.

Example:

Person A: Sǒng-sǎi bpai mâi tun nâe leuy. Person B: Ao bpen wâa...dǐao, pǒm bpai gàwn láeo gâw bpai nâng raw têe nân laéo koon kôi dtaam pǒm bpai ná.

คนแรก: สงสัยไปไม่ทันแน่เลย คนที่สอง: เอาเป็นว่าเดี๋ยวผมไปก่อนแล้วก็ไปนั่งรอที่นั่น แล้วคุณค่อยตามผมไปนะ

Person A: I don't think I am going to make it there. Person B: How about this – I'll go there first and wait and you come later.

Ao bpen wâa mun mâi châi kwaam pìt kǎwng krai mâi dtâwng tôht gun. Rêuang gèuhd láeo gâw bplòi hâi mun gèuhd bpai. Yang ngai gâw glàp bpai gâe kǎi mâi dâai yòo dee.

เอาเป็นว่ามันไม่ใช่ความผิดของใคร ไม่ต้องโทษกัน เรื่องเกิดแล้วก็ปล่อยให้มันเกิดไป ยังไงก็กลับไปแก้ไขไม่ได้อยู่ดี

Let's just say it wasn't anyone's fault – no point blaming each other. Whatever's happened has happened and we can't go back and change anything so best to let it go.

31. tâeb แทบ

Meaning – almost

Context – often used in songs e.g. "tâeb jà kàat jai", this word is another one of those that will impress listeners as most foreigners will know 'gèuap', at most, whereas 'tâeb' is a bit of a 'fancier' word. Well worth trying to practise it with a native Thai speaker.

Example:

Dta-làwt taang tâeb mâi dâi jeuh krai leuy, kôi róo-sèuk mee kwaam bpen sùan dtua nòi.

ตลอดทางแทบไม่ได้เจอใครเลย ค่อยรู้สึกมีความเป็นส่วนตัวหน่อย

I hardly came across anybody on the way and so managed to get some privacy.

Notice the use of 'kwaam'...it has been in many of the sentences already so you already should know that 'kwaam' transforms an adjective to a corresponding noun (e.g. 'kwaam chà-làat' transforms *'clever'* into *'intelligence'*).

Tâeb jà mâi lěua arai leuy.

แทบจะไม่เหลืออะไรเลย

There's hardly anything left (for example, in the store).

32. gâw leuy ก็เลย

Meaning – and so / therefore

Context – this is a less formal way of saying '*therefore*' as compared to '<u>práw</u>-<u>chà</u>-<u>nán</u>' or '<u>dang nán</u>'. The difference in usage is subtle and it takes some understanding of Thai to automatically choose the right word for the situation. For now, one way to distinguish the two is that '<u>gâw</u> leuy' is often used when telling a story or recounting what you or someone else did earlier whereas the other two more formal words are more for logical arguments or describing consequences or any follow-up. '<u>Gâw</u> leuy' is so common in everyday spoken Thai, it is well worth learning it well.

Example:

<u>Bpai</u> têe râek <u>mâi</u> mee <u>a-rai</u> tòok <u>jai</u> <u>gâw</u> leuy <u>kíd</u> wâa <u>wái</u> <u>bpai</u> doo têe '<u>Cen-tûn</u>' (Central Department Store) dee gwàa.

ไปที่แรกไม่มีอะไรถูกใจก็เลยคิดว่าไว้ไปดูที่เซ็นทรัลดีกว่า

I didn't see anything I liked at the first place so I think it might be better to go and take a look in Central Department Store.

Did you notice the expression '<u>tòok jai</u>' – literally '*touched my heart*'? A good alternative to saying 'châwp'.

Mêua cháao jeuh săao nâa-rák bon rót fai fáa dtâai din; káo sòng yím hâi pŏm, pŏm gâw leuy yím glàp. Sĭa daai, pŏm tĕung sà-tăa-nee têe jà long reo bpai nòi, leuy mâi dâi kăw beuh.

เมื่อเช้าเจอสาวน่ารักบนรถไฟฟ้าใต้ดิน เขาส่งยิ้มให้ผมผมก็เลยยิ้มกลับ เสียดายผมถึงสถานีที่จะลงเร็วไปหน่อยเลยไม่ได้ขอเบอร์

This morning I met a cute girl on the underground; she smiled at me and so I smiled back. (It's a) shame I reached my stop so soon and didn't get a chance to get her number.

'mêua' is a better word to use than 'dtawn' as it is used more when the specific time of the thing you are talking about is not very important to the meaning. But, having said that, if you had used 'dtawn' in the above sentence, it would not be wrong.

Notice that 'gâw leuy' is shortened to just 'leuy', which is fine.

> **Tips / in my experience / insight:** *It was probably a good thing he reached his stop as it probably prevented him from embarrassing himself – Thailand is not the place to openly approach people in public. But, hey, if you want to give it a go, the word you need is 'kăw beuh' and add 'nòi' to soften it and of course the obligatory 'krúp'. 'beuh' is just 'number'. To be honest, these days you are probably better off asking to connect on LINE, which doesn't require the other person to give you their number. If you want to try...say "mâi sâap wâa chái LINE yòo rĕu bplào krúp?" and take it from there. Good luck (Chôhk dee!)!*

33. dtòk-long ตกลง

Meaning – so / in the end

Context – one of the more difficult words to use properly in Thai and therefore, all the more worthwhile learning in order to get major credit from local speakers. 'dtòk-long' does mean 'so' but it is quite different to 'dang nán' or 'gâw leuy'. The literal meaning is 'agree' and this gives an indication to its use; it basically means "so, are we agreed on...?" Usually it is used when you have discussed some options already but no decision has been made yet or there is an ongoing discussion and you want to bring it to a head and decide on a course of action or you want to summarise next steps etc.

Example:

Dtòk-long jà bpai năi gun?

ตกลงจะไปไหนกัน

So where (have we decided we are) / are we going?

You have to add the 'gun' if you mean going together somewhere.

Dtòk-long dtaam née ná.

ตกลงตามนี้นะ

Ok, so we'll go ahead as we've just discussed.

Dtòk-long jà ao yang ngai gun nâe? Jà bpai 'drĭng' (drink) gun gàwn mái laéo kôi bpai gin kâao gun.

ตกลงจะเอายังไงกันแน่ จะไปดริ๊งค์กันก่อนไหม แล้วค่อยไปกินข้าวกัน

So what do you all want to do? Shall we go and get a few drinks first and then get some food afterward?

In the above sentence, the 'nâe', which means *'certain'* or *'sure'* makes the question a bit more 'girly' or 'whiny' but not excessively so.

BTW, you could always say ~~deum~~ instead of the Thai version of *'drink'* if you wanted to. As you will have noticed, there are many English words used colloquially in Thai, complete with Thai pronunciation and this book contains many of these. Strictly speaking these are not really slang words but clearly many of these are not so acceptable in formal conversation.

> **Tips / in my experience / insight:** *I often use this word, not just because I am not all that easy-going and like a bit of certainty and direct conversation (and so Thailand is sometimes a struggle even though I am fluent!), but also in situations like when I have listened to a meeting or watched the news and understood it vaguely and then ask whoever I am with "**dtòk-long bprà-den keu**..."or "**dtòk-long mun** măai kwaam wâa..." etc.*
>
> *BTW, **dtòk-long** can also be used as part of a noun such as 'kâw **dtòk-long**' which means a '**statement or document of agreement**'. You will hear it in TV programmes on current affairs or politics.*

34. dtaai laéo! ตายแล้ว!

Meaning – Oh my god!

Context – as you can see from the indicator, this word is given the highest 'feminine' rating because it is really only used by women or well...others who are effeminate shall we say. Literally it means "*I've just died*" and it is an overly dramatic expression to exclaim surprise. It is actually a lot of fun to say and the more sing-song you say it, the more fun and funny it sounds. If you are male and confident enough in your masculinity, feel free to give it a go if you are with some female friends – you are bound to get some giggles, especially if you have heard it from an actor on TV playing a gay character and managed to copy the sound accurately. Obviously, for women, this is just a normal word to show surprise and help you bond with your girlfriends.

Example:

Ooi dtaai laéo teuh, <u>chún</u> <u>mâi</u> glâa <u>tam</u> <u>yàng</u> teuh ràwk <u>ná</u>, <u>jà</u> bàwk <u>hâi</u>.

โอ้ย ตายแล้วเธอ ฉันไม่กล้าทำอย่างเธอหรอกนะ จะบอกให้

Omg! I would never dare do that, (I'm telling you)!

'teuh' and other pronouns will be in the next book.

'glâa' means 'brave'.

Ooi, dtaai laéo, <u>mâi</u> jeuh <u>dtâng</u> naan, sŭay <u>kê~~u~~n</u> <u>dtâng</u> yéuh.

โอ้ยตายแล้ว ไม่เจอตั้งนานสวยขึ้นตั้งเยอะ

Hey, I haven't seen you for ages, you are looking great!

The use of '<u>dtâng</u>' makes this an even more 'girly' sentence. A more realistic translation would be something like "*Oh darling, you are looking fabulous…*".

Tips / in my experience / insight: *try watching 'Săam <u>Sâep</u>' with Caramae (on Youtube if it is not on TV) – she says this word a lot, with some short ones and other longer, more dramatic ones. Very amusing! If you are male, try going to a café with your Thai friends and use this word loudly – if you copied the sound dramatically enough, you are bound to get a reaction. Perhaps best not used in the classroom (if you are a teacher) or even in the staff room when something surprising happens, unless you are confident people will get your sense of humour!*

Another similar expression that you are bound to hear from women is '<u>jà</u> bâa dtaai' – literally translating as 'I'll go so crazy, I'm gonna die'. Again, not really advisable for men to use this expression – although it is a bit less feminine than 'dtaai láeo', it is not really something men use as much as women. When you are more comfortable with Thai you can make your own judgements.

Just like other words I have labelled as feminine, obviously these are just opinions to give some guidelines and insight and obviously there is no official policy on what words a man can use and what words a woman can use – that would clearly be utterly ridiculous. I am simply advising that generally men's language is a little less flamboyant and emotional than women's so if you care about how you come across, try to notice how the genders differ in their style of speech when you are in Thailand.

35. kôi kôi ค่อย ๆ

Meaning – gradually / little by little

Context – many words in Thai are twinned and this is one example; in this case, the purpose and meaning is exactly as in English – *'little by little'*. It can also be used to describe things being done slowly or encourage taking your time.

Example:

Kôi kôi kíd laéo kôi dtàt-sĭn jai.

ค่อย ๆ คิด แล้วค่อยตัดสินใจ

Think it through and then decide.

Káo kôi kôi deuhn mĕuan kon gàe.

เขาค่อย ๆ เดินเหมือนคนแก่

He walks slowly (shuffles along) like an old person.

36. dtàw bpai ต่อไป

Meaning – in the future / next

Context – similar to English, it can be used specifically as '*next*' or more abstractly or philosophically as '*in the future*'.

Example:

Dtawn née róo wâa tam dtua mâi kôi dee dtàw bpai jà tam dtua dee gwàa née.

ตอนนี้รู้ว่าทำตัวไม่ค่อยดี ต่อไปจะทำตัวดีกว่านี้

I know I haven't been behaving well these days. I'll do better in the future / next time (a sentence which, admittedly, sounds a little odd in English).

Kráng dtàw bpai yàak jà bpai tîao Gàw Similan...wâa ngai, yàak bpai mái?

ครั้งต่อไปอยากจะไปเที่ยวเกาะสิมิลัน... ว่าไง อยากไปไหม

Next time I want to go to Similan Island...what do you think, want to go?

> **Tips / in my experience / insight:** There is no excuse for not knowing the word '*dtàw bpai*' if you have spent any time in Bangkok as it is part of every announcement coming up to a stop: "*sa-tăa-nee dtàw bpai*...".

37. kon lá rêuang / kon / bprà-den

คนละเรื่อง / คน / ประเด็น

Meaning – a whole different story / person / point

Context – 'kon lá' means 'else' or 'different' e.g. 'someone else'. If you want to say that two things are different, you can use 'dtàang gun' but 'kon lá rêuang' is used when you want to intensify the difference. 'kon lá rêuang' is quite a common word meaning 'a whole different story' or similar i.e. when you want to say that the thing you are referring to is completely in a different league or whole different ballgame to what the other person refers to. You can also use it to refer to a point you are making being a different point to the point being made by someone else so when they give their view, you preface your response by stating that your point is 'kon lá bprà-den'.

Example:

Person A: Nân kon têe teuh pôod tĕung mêua chaáo mâi châi lĕuh? Person B: Mâi châi, nân mun kon lá kon gun, kon têe chún pôod tĕung mâi châi kon nán.

คนแรก: นั่นคนที่เธอพูดถึงเมื่อเช้าไม่ใช่เหรอ คนที่สอง: ไม่ใช่ นั่นมันคนละคนกัน คนที่ฉันพูดถึงไม่ใช่คนนั้น

Person A: That's the person you were talking about this morning, right? Person B: No, that's not him, that's somebody else, the person I was talking about is not that guy.

Pák rohng raem tăeo née gùp pák rá-dàp hâa daao rim mâe náam nêe mun kon lá rêuang – tîap gun mâi dâai leuy.

พักโรงแรมแถวนี้กับพักระดับห้าดาวริมแม่น้ำนี่มันคนละเรื่อง เทียบกันไม่ได้เลย

You can't compare a hotel around here to a five star Riverside hotel – it's on a completely different scale!

'rá-dàp' means '*level*' and can be used for many situations where status or rank or quality is the point e.g. 'bâan rá-dàp săwng láan' **means** '*houses around the two million mark*' and so on.

Mâi dâi pôod tĕung rêuang nán – pôod tĕung kon lá bprà-den. Keu yàng née...

ไม่ได้พูดถึงเรื่องนั้น พูดถึงคนละประเด็น คืออย่างนี้...

No, that wasn't what I was talking about – my point was something else. Let me explain (in literal terms – "the thing is...").

> **Tips / in my experience / insight:** *You will hear* '*kon lá rêuang*' *used for many things, not just to do with scale but almost anything that is significantly different e.g. requires much more effort could be* '*kon lá rêuang*' *to whatever you were discussing initially, which presumably is much easier. See? Learn to use this and you are on your way to real spoken Thai. But be careful in how you use it as it can be quite a forceful expression...you'll get the feel of it.*
>
> *BTW, in case it wasn't obvious, it is only* '*kon lá rêuang*' *that I have labelled as a very low ranking blunt expression, not the other two words in the title.*

38. rĕu bplào หรือเปล่า

Meaning – or not

Context – in English this word would be considered a bit rude e.g. "*do you want to go or not?*" but in Thai, it is slightly less so, especially if you add the normal '<u>krúp</u>' or '<u>kà</u>' at the end. 'Rĕu bplào' is an alternative to '<u>mái</u>' and offers a bit more directness in the question without being confrontational. Note that it can also be used in a similar way to English when you are making a statement (as opposed to asking a question), such as "*we do not know whether...or not*".

Example:

<u>Wan</u> née mee 'cláat' (class) dtawn bàai rĕu bplào?

วันนี้มี 'คลาส' ตอนบ่ายรึเปล่า

Do you have any classes in the afternoon today?

Person A: <u>Mâi</u> sâap wâa <u>sŏn</u> <u>jai</u> <u>jà</u> <u>bpai</u> taan kâao dûai <u>gan</u> <u>mái</u> <u>krúp</u>? Person B: Aăw, <u>kà</u>, <u>bpai</u> <u>kà</u>. Person A: Keuy <u>bpai</u> ráan Krua Náam <u>Dtòk</u> rĕu bplaao <u>krúp</u>? Person B: <u>Mâi</u> keuy <u>kà</u>. Yàak <u>bpai</u>.

คนแรก: ไม่ทราบว่าสนใจจะไปทานข้าวด้วยกันไหมครับ คนที่สอง: อ๋อ คะ ไป คะ คนแรก: เคยไปร้านครัวน้ำตกหรือเปล่าครับ คนที่สอง: ไม่เคยคะ อยากไป

Person A: I was wondering whether you wanted to go out to dinner. Person B: Oh, yes, sure. Person A: Have you ever been to the Waterfall Restaurant? Person B: No, never but I would like to.

39. k~~eu~~ / gâw k~~eu~~ wâa คือ / ก็คือว่า

Meaning – it is / it's like this...

Context – another common word in spoken Thai and often used to start sentences when you want to explain something and you are building up to your explanation...in other words, it's often a word for stalling or providing a suitable pause or rhythm.

Example:

K~~eu~~...mun bpen yàng ngée...

คือ... มันเป็นยังงี้...

See...it's like / the situation is like this...

K~~eu~~ jà kíd yàng nán gâw mâi tòok; mun mâi châi kwaam pìt kăwng káo.

คือ จะคิดอย่างนั้นก็ไม่ถูก มันไม่ใช่ความผิดของเขา

Erm, that's not really fair to be honest, I mean it's not his fault.

Tips / in my experience / insight: *In Thai you will sometimes hear two or three sets of 'gâw k~~eu~~'s, where each is slightly closer to what the person is actually trying to explain but either is incapable of being more direct the first time or is starting off understated and slowly building up to what he / she really means. Sometimes this can be quite frustrating for a Western mindset.*

40. laéo yang ngai / ngai dtàw
แล้วยังไง / ไงต่อ

Meaning – and then? / so?

Context – this is slightly direct, as it is in English but doesn't necessarily have to be – it depends on the context and the tone you use.

Example:

Person A: Pêung kui gùp pêuan. Káo lâo rêuang têe káo bpai Canada maa... Person B: Laéo ngai?

คนแรก: เพิ่งคุยกับเพื่อน เขาเล่าเรื่องที่เขาไปแคนาดามา... คนที่สอง: แล้วไง

Person A: I was just talking to my friend and he was telling me about his trip to Canada... Person B: Yeah, and...?

The phrase 'lâo rêuang' is a bit of a casual expression but is perfectly fine to use in everyday conversation. It is an alternative to 'bàwk'.

Note that 'laéo ngai' also means '*so what?*'

(Passenger to taxi driver) Person A: Dtâwng líao kwăa laéo kùp dtrong bpai rêuay rêuay... Person B: Laéo ngai dtàw?

คนแรก: ต้องเลี้ยวขวาแล้วขับตรงไปเรื่อย ๆ .... คนที่สอง: แล้วไงต่อ

Person A: You need to turn right and then straight on for a while. Person B: Ok and then what?

41. mâi kôi dâai ไม่ค่อยได้ S

Meaning – can't really...

Context – the '_kôi_' tones down cannot to '_cannot quite_' or similar.

Example:

Dǐao née gin kâao mâi kôi dâai měuan sà-mǎi gàwn láeo... jam dâai wâa sìp gwàa bpee têe laéo, we-laa bpai gin kâao gùp pêuan pôo-chaai dtàang kon dtàang sàng kâao mâi dtùm gwàa sǎam jaan...baang tee, sèe, hâa jaan gâw mee!

เดี๋ยวนี้กินข้าวไม่ค่อยได้เหมือนสมัยก่อนแล้ว จำได้ว่าสิบกว่าปีที่แล้ว เวลาไปกินข้าวกับเพื่อนผู้ชายต่างคนต่างสั่งข้าวไม่ต่ำกว่าสามจาน บางทีสี่ห้าจานก็มี

I can't really put away food like I used to be able to. I remember over ten years ago, I used to go out to eat with a male friend and we would both have at least three plates of rice...sometimes even four or five!

Notice the use of sà-mǎi, which is a bit like saying _"in the old days"._ I have expanded on sà-mǎi a bit later in this book.

Also notice the phrase 'dtàang kon dtàang', which I could have translated as _"each of us"_ as opposed to _"both of us"_, to be a bit more accurate. 'dtàang' is the word for '_different_' so you can see how it is used to mean '_each_'.

Finally, importantly, note that when 'mâi kôi dâi' precedes a verb, it is the past tense i.e. '_did not get to_' or '_haven't had much of a chance to_' e.g. 'dǐao née mâi kôi dâi doo TV'.

42. kà-nàad nán ขนาดนั้น

Meaning – in spite of that / even if we take that into account / even then

Context – pretty much the same as 'tĕung yàng nán', the literal meaning is '*in that way*', as 'kà-nàad' means '*type*' or '*style*' or '*way*'.

Example:

Têe bâan káo mâi kôi mee ngeuhn; Tĕung kà-nàad nán káo gâw yang dtâng jai rian. Káo bàwk wâa yàak kâo 'Jòo-laa' (Chulalongkorn).

ที่บ้านเขาไม่ค่อยมีเงิน ถึงขนาดนั้นเขาก็ยังตั้งใจเรียน เขาบอกว่าอยากเข้าจุฬา

His family is not that well off but he still studies hard and he says he wants to get into Chulalongkorn University.

Try to pick up the use of 'têe bâan', which is an alternative way of saying '*family*' and if the person's parents and other relatives live outside Bangkok, it refers to them in the family home, even if the person has a flat in Bangkok because they work there.

Notice that 'dtâng jai' means '*intend*' in literal terms and is used above to mean '*study hard*'.

In normal conversation, people usually shorten the word for university from 'ma-hăa-wít-tá-yaa-lai' to 'ma-hăa-lai', or omit it completely as in the example above and just say the name of (Thailand's most elite) the university.

Finally, one thing that will get you instant credibility with Thai people is the ability to pronounce place names properly e.g. the word for island (Gàw, not Koh) and not in either an English way or following the official transliteration.

So, get your 'Bumrungrad's, 'Chulalongkorn's and your 'Suvarnabhumi's correct and you will be accepted more easily. Your alternative is to not bother, get it wrong, still be understood after some confusion and then be thought of as a foreigner who can't really speak Thai so need to be spoken to in English.

> **Cultural insight / life in Thailand: Tone yourself down a tad**
>
> *So you shouldn't try to be more Thai than Thai people but fit in with Thai people but also be yourself...confused? Don't worry, it's not a formula and there are no rules here. These are just insights to help you understand what you are experiencing and likely to experience in Thailand. You are free to disregard these and go your own way.*
>
> *But assuming you are interested, this one is about being little less conspicuous, a little less opinionated, less confrontational if you possibly can. You might think that this amounts to you not being you so I will leave you to decide how much of this adjustment is palatable to you and your own sense of self.*
>
> *The point is you are in a foreign country and a country where there is a lot of subtlety and subtext (as indeed there is in English society) and so it is best to listen first, be humble and comment later.*
>
> *One final point that may seem a bit strange to mention in this context – there is no need to say "Sa-wàt-dee krúp" to everyone every morning. It's not wrong per se but you will notice that Thais do not uphold this custom as rigorously as in the West. Often Thais will say "bpen ngai" or just launch into conversation. Similarly, there is no tradition of asking what you did on the weekend, if you are in an office environment, on a Monday morning.*

43. châi mái là?! ใช่ไหมล่ะ

Meaning – right?! / am I right or what?

Context – the addition of 'là' makes this a slightly more direct version of 'châi mái'. It is often used when you want to show a hint of sarcasm or use a slightly challenging tone, like, for example when the thing you are referring to is quite obviously true. Note that this does not necessarily mean that 'châi mái là' is an overtly aggressive word as it is often used when both people actually agree on the speaker's point of view anyway. So it is not a case of challenging the other person in some cases as much as being a bit more direct and making the point a bit more poignantly or humorously. Again, one of those words where you need to have experience of being in Thai society to be able to use this word appropriately without causing offence. Hence, a word that offers a challenge but rewards once learnt!

Example:

Hiǔw kâao châi mái là? Dâi yin táwng ráwng siǎng dang chiao.

หิวข้าวใช่ไหมล่ะ ได้ยินท้องร้องเสียงดังเซียว

You're hungry, right? I can hear your belly rumbling so loudly.

Notice the teasing nature of the sentence, which is made a little more feminine with the use of 'chiao'.

Also notice that the English translation doesn't really take account of the 'là'; I could have translated it as '*I bet you're hungry aren't you?*', which would be closer to the sentiment of the Thai.

Mun mâi ngâai kà-nàad nán châi mâi là; yàak bpai tîao měuan gun dtàe chûang née ngaan yôong. Gwàa jà laa ngaan daai gâw kong dtâwng raw èeg săwng săam deuan. Ao yàng née taen mái, săo aa-tít nâa rao bpai tîao Hŭa-Hĭn gun? Mâi glai mâak; baang tee, àad-jà laa wan sòok dâai dûai – bpai yòo săam wan leuy.

มันไม่ง่ายขนาดนั้นใช่ไหมล่ะ อยากไปเที่ยว
เหมือนกันแต่ช่วงนี้งานยุ่ง กว่าจะลางานได้ก็
คงต้องรออีกสองสามเดือน เอาอย่างนี้แทนไหม
เสาร์อาทิตย์หน้าเราไปเที่ยวหัวหินกัน ไม่ไกลมาก
บางทีอาจจะลาวันศุกร์ได้ด้วย ไปอยู่สามวันเลย

It's not that simple is it – I want to go on holiday too but these days I am quite busy at work and so by the time I can take any time off work, it will be probably be another two or three months. How about this instead, how about going to Hua Hin next weekend? It's less travelling and maybe I could even take Friday off and we can go go for three days? Sound good?

Try to practise saying lengthy pieces of conversation such as the one above. Your confidence will increase massively when you can get through three or four sentences in a row and be understood and the listener responds accordingly without switching to English. Now you are on your way to fluency.

> **Tips / in my experience / insight:** *I tend to use this with people close to me but would never go round Bangkok using this instead of '__châi mái__', especially with people I do not know so be careful! With people close to you, it is perfectly acceptable though, like if your wife is sitting in aircon and you've just returned from outside all hot and sweaty and she would say…"ah, you're hot now aren't you" and that goes double if you had said before leaving, overconfidently, you would be fine even if you walk, as opposed to taking a taxi. See how it is used?*

44. mĕuan gùp wâa เหมือนกับว่า

Meaning – it's like / seems like / it's almost as if

Context – one of the many useful words to those speakers who want to progress beyond intermediate level, this literally translates as '*it is similar with*'. You can use this word in a multitude of different situations and it will allow you to express concepts more colourfully than simple textbook language, which is surely not what you want to use around Thailand.

Example:

Person A: Mĕuan wâa dĭao née krai krai gâw bpen kroo săwn paa-săa ang-grìt dâai. Kâeh bpen 'farang' gâw paw laéo. Person B: Mâi jing ràwk! Pûak rohng rian káo gâw dtâwng mee mâat-dtrà-tăan nai gaan rúp kroo sì.

คนแรก: เหมือนว่าเดี๋ยวนี้ใครๆก็เป็นครูสอนภาษาอังกฤษได้ แค่เป็นฝรั่งก็พอแล้ว

คนที่สอง: ไม่จริงหรอก พวกโรงเรียนเขาก็ต้องมีมาตรฐานในการรับครูสิ

Person A: Seems like anybody can be an English teacher these days – all you need to do is be a foreigner. Person B: That's not true at all. Every school has minimum standards for teachers who apply.

Notice the use of the 'ràwk' even when, or perhaps, especially because the sentence is a firm rebuttal, the 'ràwk' softens it – see later in this book.

45. jà dâi... จะได้

Meaning – so that... / in order to

Context – a very easy and commonly used word to learn.

Example:

Yàak jà těung bâan reo reo jung jà dâi doo 'bàwn' (football).

อยากจะถึงบ้านเร็ว ๆ จัง จะได้ดูบอล

I want to get home quickly so that I can catch the football.

> **Cultural insight / life in Thailand: Respect local customs**
>
> Yes this is obvious but I still felt it worth saying since the very fact that I have listed these alternative cultural insights should not imply in the slightest that you should ignore the traditional pillars of Thai cultural concepts. These are paramount and your respect for them should be to the utmost.
>
> So, ensuring you do not make others lose face in public, recognizing when someone is not being communicative because they are worried about their English ability or they are trying to save you face (as bizarre as that sounds), being patient and not losing your temper, being open minded and thoughtful toward others, having consideration for others' situation (*greng jai*) are the essence of being Thai.
>
> Sometimes some of these can be infuriating for a Western mindset where the ability to deal with things calmly but openly and directly is a virtue and problem resolution by frank discussion is encouraged. Thais may even lie to save you face but just accept it and move on.

46. chôhk dee โชคดี

Meaning – good luck

Context – you probably already know this word but you may not know that it can be used in more situations than just where the person being spoken to is about to do something that would specifically benefit from luck. For example, you can say it to taxi drivers instead of goodbye. Saying "goodbye" is a bit weird after a short taxi ride and you do not even know the driver personally, whereas saying 'chôhk dee' is a warmer regard and doesn't necessarily mean you are wishing the person luck in the sense that Westerners would understand i.e. for some specific activity.

Example:

Person A: Sèe sìp hâa bàht krúp. Person B: Kàwb koon krúp. Chôhk dee krúp.

คนแรก: สี่สิบห้าบาทครับ คนที่สอง: ขอบคุณครับ โชคดีครับ

Person A: 45 baht please. Person B: Thanks. Good luck.

A reminder that I have used 'krúp' here explicitly but not throughout simply because it would clutter the sentences to write 'krúp' / 'kà' everywhere but in real life you have to use these words at the end of your sentence. I am sure you know this but just in case…don't copy and say without adding 'krúp' / 'kà' when directing a sentence or question at someone. You will get a feel for it in time; when in doubt default to politeness.

47. sà-măi nán / née สมัยนั้น

Meaning – in those days / these days

Context – 'sà-măi nán' is generally used when the period of time is a long time ago. Often it is intentionally used to subtly overstate how long ago something was to make the point that things were different back in the day compared to now. If you are young, obviously it will sound a little ridiculous to use 'sà-măi' unless you can pull it off in a tongue-in-cheek tone.

Example:

Sà-măi nán jam dâai wâa dtèun dtên gùp tóok yàang nai chee-wít têe meuang tai.

สมัยนั้น จำได้ว่าตื่นเต้นกับทุกอย่างในชีวิตที่เมืองไทย

I remember in those days I was so excited about everything to do with life in Thailand.

Nêe bpen pleng dtawn sà-măi têe pŏm yòo meuang tai.

นี่เป็นเพลงตอนสมัยที่ผมอยู่เมืองไทย

This is a song from the time I used to live here (in Thailand).

Learning Thai from songs is one of the best ways. There are many sites that list songs with translations in English and karaoke (transliterated Thai). Not only will your language improve, you will also have a way to connect to Thai people outside of work – if you can sing even a few lines of a popular Thai song, you are absolutely guaranteed massive kudos.

48. taen têe jà แทนที่จะ

Meaning – instead of

Context – just as in English, where the word 'taen' means 'instead' or 'exchange'. Do you know what the word for 'agent' is – it is 'dtua taen'.

Example:

Taen têe jà bpai taang nán rao săa-mâad kêun taang dùan dâai.

แทนที่จะไปทางนั้น เราสามารถขึ้นทางด่วนได้

Instead of going that way we can go by the tollway.

'dùan' means '*urgent*'. You can use 'dùan' in several ways; for example, 'dtâwng kâo hâwng náam. Dùan!' – '*I need to go to the toilet right now!*'. 'Sòng dùan' means to send by express delivery.

Hĕn jai káo bâang sì; taen têe jà wâa káo dtà-làwd lawng kít jàak môom mawng káo doo bâang.

เห็นใจเขาบ้างสิ แทนที่จะว่าเขาตลอด ลองคิดจากมุมมองเขาดูบ้าง

Give him a break – instead of having a go at him all the time why don't you stop and try and see things from his perspective first.

49. jon (tĕung) / jon gwàa จนถึง / จนกว่า

Meaning – until / until after

Context – the 'tĕung' can sometimes be left out for short and it still means 'until' or 'to the point'.

Example:
Pŏm tam jon glài jà bpen pôo chîao-chaan bpai laéo.

ผมทำจนใกล้จะเป็นผู้เชี่ยวชาญไปแล้ว

I've been doing it so long I am almost an expert

The sentence literally translated woud be 'until I am almost an expert'. 'Glài jà bpen' is a good phrase to learn and sounds like the kind of thing a new learner would not know so use it to impress other with your skills.

Tam ngaan bpen kroo săwn paa-săa ang-grìt gâw dee ná – ngeuhn deuan gâw dee laéo ngaan gâw mâi mĕuan gun tóok wan. Kíd wâa kong jà mâi bplian ngaan laéo là, jà tam jon gwàa jà glàp bprà-têt.

ทำงานเป็นครูสอนภาษาอังกฤษก็ดีนะ เงินเดือนก็ดี แล้วงานก็ไม่เหมือนกันทุกวัน คิดว่าคงจะไม่เปลี่ยนงานแล้วล่ะ จะทำจนกว่าจะกลับประเทศ

Being an English teacher is quite good – the pay is good and there is variety in the work day to day. I think I will carry on with it until I go back home (to my country) (rather than try and find some other type of job here).

50. pôod tĕung (wâa)

Meaning – talking about that… / now that you mention that

Context – this works in a similar way to English and is useful if you want to sound natural in your spoken Thai and blend into a conversation.

Example:

Pôod tĕung wâa wan née bpen wan gèuhd kăwng náwng ná.

พูดถึงว่าวันนี้เป็นวันเกิดของน้องนะ

Talking about (that or him), today is his / her birthday you know?

Person A: Gin pèt dâai mái? Person B: Mâi kôi dâai ràwk. Gin gaeng kĕe-o wăan gâw pèt mâak láeo săm-rùp chún, sôm-dtum mâi dtâwng pôod tĕung.

คนแรก: กินเผ็ดได้ไหม คนที่สอง: ไม่ค่อยได้หรอก แค่แกงเขียวหวานก็เผ็ดมากแล้วยิ่งสำหรับฉัน ส้มตำไม่ต้องพูดถึง

Person A: Are you ok with spicy food? Person B: Not really to be honest. Even green curry is way too spicy for me, never mind papaya salad.

51. súk wan (neung) สักวัน

Meaning – (just) one day (you'll see)

Context – this expression can come off a bit dramatic and in Thai sounds a bit more feminine than an 'average' word. In essence it means *'there will be a day when...'* so I have translated the meaning as above to indicate that it doesn't just mean one day in a neutral sense.

Example:

Dĭao súk wan neung jà tam hâi doo.

เดี๋ยวสักวันหนึ่งจะทำให้ดู

I'll make it one day, you wait and see.

Person A: Chái we-laa naan mái? Person B: Mâi naan ràwk, súk wan, săwng wan gâw sèt laéo.

คนแรก: ใช้เวลานานไหม คนที่สอง: ไม่นานหรอกสักวันสองวันก็เสร็จแล้ว

Person A: Will it take long? Person B: No, not long, we'll be done in approximately a couple of days.

In the above sentence without the 'neung' at the end and where it is part of the phrase 'súk wan, săwng wan' it just reverts to a normal phrase without any melodramatic overtone and the 'súk' means *'approximately'* or *'around'*..

52. wan dtàw maa วันต่อมา

Meaning – the next day

Context – no, it does not mean '*tomorrow*', it refers to the next day when that day is in the past e.g. when you are recounting an occurrence.

Example:

Wan sòok bpai tîao 'pùb' maa – mun mâak leuy, dèum yéuh! Wan dtàw maa bpùat hŭa yàng raeng.

วันศุกร์ไปเที่ยวผับมา มันมากเลยดื่มเยอะ วันต่อมาปวดหัวอย่างแรง

I went to a great bar on Friday...had loads to drink and had a lot of fun. The next day though I got a massive headache.

Although I have used 'wan dtàw maa', in casual conversation, it may be more common to hear the expression 'wan rôong kêun'.

The word 'mun' here means '*fun*' – it is a more casual word than 'sà-nòok'.

Be careful with 'yàng raeng', as I explain later in this book – it is a bit of a 'rough' expression.

53. krai gâw mâi róo ใครก็ไม่รู้

Meaning – don't know who that is / don't recognize that person

Context – this expression is quite useful because the use of 'gâw' and the rhythm of the words ending in 'róo', which can be slightly emphasized and extended in pronunciation, can all contribute to making it a bit more of a direct expression. This makes it also slightly amusing and approximates to "*I don't know who the hell that is*" or "*I have no idea who that is*" and so is a good expression to try to get a smile or a giggle (if you say it with mock aggression) and make people warm to you.

Example:

Hĕn kon nán tăeo née lăai kráng laéo; krai gâw mâi róo.

เห็นคนนั้นแถวนี้หลายครั้งแล้ว ใครก็ไม่รู้

I've seen that guy around here many times, no idea who he is!

You can use 'gâw mâi róo' in lots of expressions. For example:

tam a-rai gâw mâi róo – *have no idea why you / he did that*

bpai năi gâw mâi róo – *have no idea where we / you are going*

kít a-rai gâw mâi róo – *how could you even think that?*

lên a-rai gâw mâi róo – *what are you playing at?*

doo tam-mai gâw mâi róo – *dunno know why we bothered watching that (film, for example)*

54. yòo têe / (mun) mâi dâi yòo têe

อยู่ที่ / ไม่ได้อยู่ที่

Meaning – is / it's to do with / it is because

Context – just as in English you can say *'is'* in many ways depending on the context, so it is in Thai. In literal terms this word translates to *'located at'*. Often instead of saying something is e.g. using 'keu', you can use 'yòo têe', which, in the right context, can help to give a hint of an underlying problem why something is not getting done, as shown in the example below.

Example:

Bprà-den yòo têe dtâwng tam a-rai, mâi châi wâa krai jà tam.

ประเด็นอยู่ที่ต้องทำอะไร ไม่ใช่ว่าใครจะทำ

The point is what we need to do, not who is going to do it.

Mun mâi dâi yòo têe káo. Káo mâi mee am-nâad nai rêuang née.

มันไม่ได้อยู่ที่เขา เขาไม่มีอำนาจในเรื่องนี้

It's nothing do with him / not stuck because of him. He can't do anything about it.

In literal terms 'am-nâad' means *'power'*.

55. kêun yòo gùp ขึ้นอยู่กับ

Meaning – it depends on / it's to do with

Context – similar to English, this is a fairly straightforward word.

Example:

Gaan têe rao jà bprà-sòp kwaam săm-rèd nai chee-wít tam ngaan mun kêun yòo gùp lăai yàang.

การที่เราจะประสบความสำเร็จในชีวิตทำงานมันขึ้นอยู่กับหลายอย่าง

Success in your career depends on many things.

Practise 'gaan têe...' and see if you can use it when appropriate in a conversation. It is harder than you think so you need to be brave and be prepared to make mistakes.

'bprà-sòp' means *'experience'* in verb form and can come off a bit formal so, for example, if you were to say "yàak jà bprà-sòp sìng mài mài", it would be fine but using 'jeuh' is better. In many everyday statements that are not so grandiose, the more common 'jeuh' is used e.g. 'yàak jeuh kon mài mài...'. You couldn't really use 'bprà-sòp' in this sentence as it would sound a little weird.

'Bprà-sòp gaan' is the noun form and is used just as in English, like when talking about having experience for a job or a holiday experience.

56. aâng wâa / aâng tĕung อ้างว่า / อ้างถึง

Meaning – mention / claim / refer to

Context – the chances are you will hear this word more than you will ever have the opportunity to use it as it can be a fairly formal word. Whereas the former means to claim, the latter uses the same word in a subtly different context i.e. to refer to.

Example:

Káo aâng wâa káo mâi róo rêuang.

เขาอ้างว่าเขาไม่รู้เรื่อง

He claims he doesn't know.

Naai-yók aâng tĕung sà-tì-dtì jam-nuan núk tâwng tîao têe kâo maa nai bprà-têt tai nai bpee 2557.

นายกอ้างถึงสถิติจำนวนนักท่องเที่ยวที่เข้ามาในประเทศไทยในปี 2557

The Prime Minister referred to statistics on the number of tourists that came to Thailand in 2014.

Did you notice the Thai word for statistics, which sounds pretty much the same as the English?

Learn these types of more formal words ('jam-nuan') from watching the news.

57. laéo jà tam tam-mai / jà mee bprà-yòht a-rai?

แล้วจะทำทำไม / จะมีประโยชน์อะไร

Meaning – and why would you do that? / what's the use / point?

Context – in this expression, the addition of the word 'laéo' gives it a more direct feel, as if to say "well, what are you going to do that for?" or "what's the point of doing that?"

Example:

Tam ngaan dtem têe dtàe mâi mee krai hěn pǒn ngaan, laéo jà tam tam-mai?

ทำงานเต็มที่แต่ไม่มีใครเห็นผลงานแล้วจะทำทำไม

What's the point of working (in this job) when you work hard but nobody appreciates your hard work?

'Dtem têe' is a word you hear often in everday conversation, meaning '*to the best of my ability*'.

'pǒn ngaan' is a word you will hear in many celebrity interviews on chat shows, like 'chûang née mee pǒn ngaan a-rai bâang?" As you can see, although the literal translation is '*result of your work*' or perhaps more metaphorically, '*fruits of your labour*', you don't use the literal translation when saying the English equivalent.

58. <u>yàng</u> raeng อย่างแรง

Meaning – a lot / seriously

Context – while this word is not exactly rude, it is not recommended that you use this word apart from when you are in company whom you already know well and trust. It is a bit of a 'rough' way of intensifying your adjective and while you may well hear Thai people use it, they will know when and where it is appropriate to use a word like this and when it is better to speak more politely.

Example:

<u>Hǐuw</u> <u>yàng</u> raeng! <u>Bpai</u> <u>gin</u> kâao <u>gun</u> <u>tèuh</u>.

หิวอย่างแรง ไปกินข้าวกันเถอะ

I am starving! Let's go and eat.

Did you notice the '<u>tèuh</u>'? This is very, very common, especially with women so learn to pick it out in conversations.

<u>Mun</u> <u>mâi</u> dee <u>yàng</u> raeng.

มันไม่ดีอย่างแรง

That's seriously bad (e.g. if talking about quality of something).

Again, be very careful before deciding to use this type of expression, especially if you are expressing a negative.

59. mêua-rài jà sèt (súk tee)?
เมื่อไหร่จะเสร็จ

Meaning – when are you going to be done?

Context – this can come off quite girly but can still be used by men, especially if you are waiting for your partner to finish getting dressed so you can leave, for example. The addition of the 'súk tee' makes it a bit more 'naggy' and so you can also say it without that part if you want.

Example:

Person A: Dtàeng dtua sèt laéo, dǐao kǎw tam pǒm èeg bpáep neung. Person B: Hoo-i, mêua-rài jà sèt súk tee?

คนแรก: แต่งตัวเสร็จแล้ว เดี๋ยวขอทำผมอีกแป๊ปนึง คนที่สอง: หุย เมื่อไหร่จะเสร็จสักที

Person A: Ok I'm done getting changed, let me just do my hair quickly. Person B: Oh! When are you going to be finally done?

Learn your 'bpáep neung's and your 'súk krôo's.

Tips / in my experience… / insight: *in my case, more often than not, it is me who receives this comment rather than says it! Unless you know your companion well, clearly, you should not be using this phrase at all. Because of its bluntness perhaps you will only come across this phrase if it is you who is being waited upon!*

60. dooy ní-sǎi โดยนิสัย

Meaning – due to the nature

Context – you often hear this when Thai people are talking about the legendary Thai smile and Thai hospitality and niceness.

Example:

Châi laéo, dooy ní-sǎi kǎwng kon tai, káo yin dee jà chûai tâo têe chûai dâai.

ใช่แล้ว โดยนิสัยของคนไทย เขายินดีจะช่วยเท่าที่ช่วยได้

Yes that's right, it's in Thai people's nature to help as much as they can.

Here's a new word that you can use – 'yin dee', which by itself means 'you are welcome' and in the above example means 'happy to'…as in 'yin dee têe dâai róo jàk'.

And another useful word is 'tâo têe' – see if you can think back to all your conversations in the past few days and if you can say any of the sentences in Thai using 'tâo têe' and then go practise it.

61. èeg nòi อีกหน่อย

Meaning – soon

Context – translated literally it means '*a bit more*' and so is roughly the same as English speakers saying "*...in a bit...*".

Example:

Èeg nòi jà sŏong gwàa mâe laéo lôok.

อีกหน่อยจะสูงกว่าแม่แล้วลูก

Soon you will be taller than me you know. (Mother saying to child).

In Thai a parent or even just an older person can refer to their children or just any young people as 'lôok' in exactly the same way as the old fashioned English way of talking such as "Come now child...".

Èeg nòi jà lêuhk sòop bòo-rèe láeo. Tóok wan née gâw mâi kôi dâi sòop; kraao née jà lêuhk jing jing.

อีกหน่อยจะเลิกสูบบุหรี่แล้ว ทุกวันนี้ก็ไม่ค่อยได้สูบ คราวนี้จะเลิกจริง ๆ

Pretty soon I'm going to give up smoking. Even as things stand I don't really smoke much day-to-day but this time I'm going to give up for real.

62. dooy têe โดยที่

Meaning – such that

Context – this is quite a tricky word to get right for new learners but in most cases, it is used in the same situations as in English.

Example:

Chêua mái wâa kon rúk gun dâai dooy têe mâi keuy jeuh gun?

เชื่อไหมว่าคนรักกันได้โดยที่ไม่เคยเจอกัน

Do you believe it's possible for two people to love each other even though they have never met?

Learn to use this form of expression – 'chêua mái wâa...', 'kíd mái wâa...', 'róo mái wâa...' and so on.

Tam ngaan dooy têe mâi dtâwng nèuay mâak.

ทำงานโดยที่ไม่ต้องเหนื่อยมาก

Work without it being too tiring.

This sentence sounds a bit more weird in English than the Thai version, which is quite a normal expression...obviously when it is in context.

63. mun mâak leuy! มันมากเลย

Meaning – so much fun!

Context – a good word to use as an alternative to the word that just about every single visitor to Thailand learns within five minutes – 'sà-nòok'.

Example:

Yàak bpai tîao 'Foon Moon bpaa-dtêe' (Full Moon Party) têe Gàw Phá Ngan mái? Mun mâak leuy!

อยากไปเที่ยว'ฟูลมูนปาร์ตี้ที่'เกาะพงันไหม มันมากเลย

You want to go to the Full Moon Party at Koh Phang Ngan? It's great fun!

Dĭao née têe Groong-Têp mee ráan 'bàwd game' yéuh. Pŏm gâw keuy bpai maa kráng neung…gâw sà-nòok dee, lên 'game' gùp lăai kon têe mâi keuy róo jàk maa gàwn – sĭang dang gan hŭa ráw gan mun mâak leuy.

เดี๋ยวนี้กรุงเทพฯ มีร้าน "บอร์ดเกม" เยอะ ผมก็เคยไปมาครั้งหนึ่งก็สนุกดี เล่นเกมกับหลายคนที่ไม่เคยรู้จักมาก่อน เสียงดังกันหัวเราะกันมันมากเลย

There are quite a lot of board game cafes in Bangkok these days. I've been once before and it was actually fun – you can play games with loads of people you've just met – it's so much fun, just shouting and laughing and having a good time.

64. sa-ròop wâa สรุปว่า

Meaning – so, to summarise

Context – this is rather similar in essence to 'dtòk-long' and should be quite easy to learn to use.

Example:

Sa-ròop wâa jà ao dtaam păen (plan) deuhm châi mái?

สรุปว่าจะเอาตามแผนเดิมใช่ไหม

So we're going to go with the original plan, right?

Cultural insight / life in Thailand: Go easy on analysis.

Another trait that you may have picked up in your conversations with Thai people is that you are unlikely to have a deep or analytical discussion for very long. Generally, and yes, it is yet another generalization, Thai people will not go far into the type of political, social or economic debate that you may be used to from back home. Never mind these, even when you take a benign everday subject and muse on why it is the case and what the impact is, you are more than likely to get an ultimate remark of indifference or that is giving the person a headache and so on.

This all may sound negative but it is just another facet of cultural awareness. Thai people are often described as 'fun loving' and this is just the corollary. It does not mean that Thai people do not discuss these topics but the style is quite different to Western culture – watch Koon Săw-rá-yóot on TV. Keep things light in Thailand.

65. pôod ngâai ngâai (keu...) พูดง่าย ๆ

Meaning – to put it simply...

Context – 'ngâai' means '*easy*' as I am sure you know so this word should be pretty straightforward to use when you want to bring a meandering discussion to a slightly more direct conclusion. Often it is followed by 'keu...'.

Example:

Pôod ngâai ngâai keu yòo meuang tai sà-baai têe sòot.

พูดง่าย ๆ คืออยู่เมืองไทยสบายที่สุด

To put it simply, living in Thailand is just the best!

Notice I did not translate 'sà-baai' directly because in English, nobody would say "living in Thailand is the most comfortable" – it does not sound natural in English because English does not have the same concept of 'sà-baai' as Thai.

Pôod ngâai ngâai keu chún kêe gìat!

พูดง่าย ๆ คือฉันขี้เกียจ

Frankly speaking / to be honest, I can't be bothered.

66. pêua / pêua têe jà เพื่อ / เพื่อที่จะ

Meaning – for / in order to

Context – this is a very commonly used word and used in several ways. In the simplest form, it just means '*for*' but the addition of 'têe jà' extends it to '*for the purpose of*'.

Example:

Jà tam pêua a-rai?!

จะทำเพื่ออะไร

Why would I do that? / What am I going to do that for? / What's the point of doing that?

Admittedly, this is a pretty aggressive sentence so use with caution in terms of who you say it to and add the 'krúp' / 'kà' to ensure you mitigate the directness.

Yàak lêuhk tam ngaan reo reo née pêua têe jà dâi mee we-laa tam yàang èun têe tóok wan née mâi kôi mee o-gàat dâi tam.

อยากเลิกทำงานเร็ว ๆ นี้ จะได้มีเวลาทำอย่างอื่นที่ทุกวันนี้ไม่ค่อยมีโอกาสได้ทำ

I want to stop working soon so that I can spend my life doing all the other things that I don't get a chance to do now.

See if you can get through a fairly complicated sentence such as this. Your confidence will shoot through the roof if you can get through it unscathed and get a sensible response or question.

67. ao wái kraao nâa เอาไว้คราวหน้า

Meaning – next time / no thanks / I'll pass

Context – you probably have already learnt that 'wái' added behind words adjusts the meaning to being something more permanent or remaining in place e.g. 'kui wái' means you have already had the discussion where 'kui' just means to discuss. In the same way, 'ao wái' means something like '*let it be like this*'. The expression 'ao wái kraao naa', which is sometimes shortened in casual speech by omitting the 'ao', can be used when you are too tired or too busy or whatever to do something and so want to leave it for next time (or maybe never).

Example:

Person A: Jà bpai doo năng mái? Person B: Ooi, wan née nèuay laéo, ao wái kraao nâa dee mái?

คนแรก: จะไปดูหนังไหม คนที่สอง: โอ๊ย วันนี้ เหนื่อยแล้ว เอาไว้คราวหน้าดีไหม

Person A: Want to go watch a movie? Person B: Is it ok if we don't go today? I'm pretty tired.

> **Tips / in my experience… / insight:** *there is also a subtler meaning where it is used to politely refuse an offer without making the person 'lose face' i.e. "no thanks" is what you really mean but what you are saying is "don't worry, leave it for next time" so that you do not flatly refuse.*

68. pèua wái เผื่อไว้

Meaning – extra / just in case

Context – I listed this separately because the meaning may not be obvious from knowing 'pèua' and 'wái' separately. 'pèua wái' is used when you want to say that something is done in excess of what is required, like for example when you buy extra food just in case your flatmate is hungry or maybe not just for this meal but also for later in the day.

Example:

Person A: Tam-mai séu gùp kâao yéuh jung? Person B: Ăw, séu pèua wái.

คนแรก: ทำไมซื้อกับข้าวเยอะจัง คนที่สอง: อ๋อ ซื้อเผื่อไว้

Person A: Why did you get so much food? Person B: Oh, I got some extra (in case you were hungry).

Gèp pèua wái.

เก็บเผื่อไว้

Keep it just in case.

69. mâi dâi tam / doo/ etc. ไม่ได้ทำ / ดู

Meaning – did not do / look / etc.

Context – I thought I would include a fairly simple word in here because some readers may not be comfortable with using the past tense properly in Thai. It might help if you understand the literal translation, which is '*I did not get to… do / look*' where the '<u>dâi</u>' means '*get to*'.

Example:

Person A: Doo <u>năng</u> rêuang née ré<s>u</s> <u>yang</u>. Person B: <u>Yang</u> <u>mâi</u> <u>dâi</u> doo, <u>bpai</u> doo gan <u>mái</u>?

คนแรกซ: ดูหนังเรื่องนี้หรือยัง คนที่สอง: ยังไม่ได้ดู ไปดูกันมั้ย

Person A: Have you seen this film yet? Person B: Not yet, shall we go and watch it?

<u>Mâi</u> <u>dâi</u> <u>tam</u> naan laéo. <u>Tam</u> <u>hâi</u> doo <u>nòi</u>.

ไม่ได้ทำนานแล้ว ทำให้ดูหน่อย

I haven't done it in ages. Can you show me.

70. long meu tam eng ลงมือทำเอง

Meaning – hands on / do it yourself

Context – the word 'long' means to descend, or get off, or to lower, or put down and so you can see how this expression comes about – to 'long meu' means to put your hands into something to get involved. Similarly, 'long kǎwng' can mean when a shopkeeper stocks his shelves before opening and 'long bpoon' means when cement is put down (by a builder, I mean).

Example:

Bpò-kà-dtì pǒm bpen kon têe châwp long meu tam a-rai eng mâak gwàa.

ปกติผมเป็นคนที่ชอบลงมือทำอะไรเองมากกว่า

Normally I'm the kind of person that likes to be hands on and do things myself.

Notice that I did not translate the 'mâak gwàa' – in Thai, sometimes 'mâak gwàa' is used even when you are not comparing to someone or something else...but even in this case there is an English equivalent – "*I'm more like the kind of person who likes to be hands-on*". See? Pretty cool huh.

Tips / in my experience… / insight: 'long' can also be used in ways that may not seem obvious such as 'long chêu', which means to put your name down for something.

71. châat / lôhk née(-a) โลกนี้ / ชาตินี้

Meaning – (in) this world / (in) this life

Context – here is a rather philosophical word that can sound mildly amusing (in a good way) if a foreigner uses it well. A lot of Thai culture and sentiment can be of this type and many conversations relating to religion or world affairs etc. tend to bring up words like this.

Example:

Mâi mee têe nǎi nai lôhk née dee tâo meuang tai.

ไม่มีที่ไหนในโลกนี้ดีเท่าเมืองไทย

There is nowhere in this world as good as Thailand. / Thailand is the best!.

Châat née(-a) mâi jeuh neua kôo gâw aàd-jà jeuh châat nâa.

ชาตินี้ไม่เจอเนื้อคู่ก็อาจจะเจอชาติหน้า

Even if I don't meet my soulmate in this life, maybe I will in the next life.

72. mâi hĕn dûai ไม่เห็นด้วย

Meaning – don't agree

Context – the phrase 'hĕn dûai' literally means to see also; 'mâi hĕn dûai' is therefore to not agree. Note that to actually say 'mâi hĕn dûai' in a Thai conversation without any softeners or qualifiers is relatively rare because it is more blunt in Thai than in English, where in some cases, it may be acceptable to be clear in your opinion that you don't agree.

Example:

Aàd-jà mee lăai kon mâi hĕn dûai dtàe rao dtâwng tam dtaam têe rao chêua.

อาจจะมีหลายคนไม่เห็นด้วยแต่เราต้องทำตามที่เราเชื่อ

There may be many people who don't agree but I have to do what I believe in.

Thai is full of philosophical statements such as this and you would do well to learn and respect these sentiments.

Notice another feature of Thai that you are probably already picking up – omission of unnecessary words. In the sentence above the Thai version does not include the *'in'* from *'believe in'*.

Tâa jà hâi nâng rót tua hòk jèd chûa mohng bpai Chiang Mài là, gâw pŏm mâi hěn dûai ná. Jà bpai yòo kâeh sǎo aa-tít eng. Mâi yàak sǐa we-laa deuhn taang naan kà-nàad nán; yawm sǐa ngeuhn nâng krêuang bin dee gwàa – paeng gwàa dtàe bprà-yùd we-laa.

ถ้าจะให้นั่งรถทัวร์หกเจ็ดชั่วโมงไปเชียงใหม่ล่ะก็ ผมไม่เห็นด้วยนะ จะไปอยู่แค่เสาร์อาทิตย์เอง ไม่อยากเสียเวลาเดินทางนานขนาดนั้น ยอมเสียเงินนั่งเครื่องบินดีกว่า แพงกว่าแต่ประหยัดเวลา

I don't really agree with having to go by bus to Chiang Mai when it takes six or seven hours to get there. After all, we're only going there for a weekend so I don't want to spend that long just getting there. Better to spend a bit more and go by plane – yes, it's more expensive but saves time.

BTW, if the situation was reversed and the Thai person was being asked to go by plane, there is every chance, especially if it is a relatively young person with a modest income, that the response would be the opposite i.e. "let's go by bus". And the chances are a Thai person wouldn't go into a long explanation as above and would just say something like "mâi ao, (mun) paeng".

If they were saying it to another Thai person, all the background cultural context of not having much disposable income and not wasting money and so on would be understood implicitly so "paeng" is enough. But for foreigners, it isn't really and being this brief could lead to you being misunderstood, perhaps as a cheap, penniless Westerner or if you wanted to go by plane, as a slightly inconsiderate and 'flashy' foreigner. Either way, it goes back to the point I made right at the start that yes, you should try to sound Thai but remembering you are a foreigner speaking Thai.

73. dtòk jai / bplàek jai têe ตกใจ / แปลกใจที่

Meaning – startled / shocked / surprised that...

Context – if you have spent some time in Thailand, you have probably heard this word several times already. So I will just give you an example of how you can use it in a sentence.

Example:

Dtòk jai têe dâi yin wâa pâw kǎwng pêuan sǐa chee-wít laéo.

ตกใจที่ได้ยินว่าพ่อของเพื่อนเสียชีวิตแล้ว

I was shocked to hear that my friend's father has passed away.

'sǐa chee-wít' is an alternative to 'dtaai' in the same way that '*passed away*' is an alternative to saying '*died*'. You can shorten it to just 'sǐa' e.g. 'pâw sǐa bpen sǎam bpee laéo' – '*my father passed away three years ago*'. 'sǐa' by itself means to waste or to lose.

Bplàek jai têe mâe yang bpai 'cháwp-bpîng' (shopping) kon dǐao dâai yòo. Mâe chún yang kǎeng raeng yòo leuy ná, jà bàwk hâi.

แปลกใจที่แม่ยังไปช้อปปิ้งคนเดียวได้อยู่ แม่ฉันยังแข็งแรงอยู่เลยนะจะบอกให้

(Assuming we are talking about someone with a fairly elderly mother) I'm surprised that mum can still go shopping by herself. My mum's pretty tough I can tell you.

74. mâi hĕn bpen / mee bpan-hăa

ไม่เห็น เป็น / มี ปัญหา

Meaning – I don't see what the problem is / that's not a problem

Context – fairly simple to understand so no further explanation needed. Just be careful to use the first of the two – 'mâi hĕn bpen bpan-hăa' – wisely, to not sound too blunt or dismissive. The use of 'ná' softens the expression.

Example:

Mâi mee bpan-hăa, dĭao chún raw tăeo née lá gun.

ไม่มีปัญหา เดี๋ยวฉันรอแถวนี้ละกัน

No problem, I'll just wait around here (until you're done).

Person A: Tam yang ngai dee. Dtòk-long gùp faen wái wâa jà bpai rúp têe condo dtawn tôom neung. Person B: Gâw mâi hĕn bpen bpan-hăa – toh bpai bàwk wâa rót dtìd yòo hâi bpai jeuh gun têe rohng năng leuy dee mái?

คนแรก: ทำยังไงดี ตกลงกับแฟนไว้ว่าจะไปรับที่คอนโดตอนทุ่มหนึ่ง คนที่สอง: ก็ไม่เห็นเป็นปัญหา โทรไปบอกว่ารถติดอยู่ ให้ไปเจอกันที่โรงหนังเลยดีไหม

Person A: I'm not going to make it. What am I going to do – I've agreed to drive over to her condo and pick her up there. Person B: I don't really see what the big deal is – just call her and tell her the traffic is really bad and this time, can you meet at the cinema.

75. tam tóo-rá ทำธุระ

Meaning – do errands / do 'stuff'

Context – this is a very common word and again, if you have spent time talking to Thai people, you are bound to have heard this word. This is one of the words in Thai where it can mean multiple things and can be deliberately vague and generic...to the point where, in some cases, the speaker doesn't actually want to tell you what specifically they are going to do so uses 'tóo-rá' to avoid telling you. For example, if you ask a girl out on a date and she doesn't want to go, she might use her long list of 'errands' as an excuse to decline. Or, of course, she actually may well be busy. Note that in the same way, it can also be a polite, indirect way of saying 'doing a no. 2 on the toilet'!

Example:

Person A: Prôong née wâang mái? Person B: Mâi wâang, prôong née mee tóo-rá.

คนแรก: พรุ่งนี้ว่างไหม คนที่สอง: ไม่ว่าง พรุ่งนี้มีธุระ

Person A: Are you free tomorrow? Person B: Sorry no, tomorrow I'm busy.

Tips / in my experience... / insight: *try this word out the next time someone asks you to go somewhere or what you did on the weekend or whatever and you do not really want to say, either because it's too many things to list or you actually do not want people knowing your business or maybe you actually were doing errands!! See the reaction you get...if you are male and speaking with a female Thai person, maybe you'll get a slightly bemused, frustrated look at getting an unsatisfactory response, especially if you continue to say '<u>tóo-rá</u>' or generally avoid revealing what you did.*

In my own experience, being a foreigner meant I got asked, often quite directly, what I did on the weekend and suchlike, whereas when I asked the same question of my Thai colleagues, I would often get vague responses.

Of course, part of the reason for this is also that, in many cases, people were just at home but it is definitely true that, for example, those that spent the weekend with their girlfriend or boyfriend or doing other personal things did not necessarily want to discuss this with people at work, especially a foreigner. So, '<u>tóo-rá</u>' is a nice convenient catch-all expression.

The Western culture of asking on a Monday morning what your colleagues did over the weekend is not really so prevalent in Thai society, apart from maybe where Westerners have influenced Thai office culture over many years. Either way, this is a good word to know.

76. mâi sà-dùak ไม่สะดวก

Meaning – not convenient / I would rather not

Context – and here is another word that again demonstrates the subtleties of Thai and the subtext behind some standard responses. Again, well worth taking time to pay attention to Thai conversation and learning to contextualize these types of words and also use them yourself – you will get real and warm appreciation that separates you from the average foreigner who speaks some Thai. In many cases this word does just mean the literal meaning i.e. not convenient but in many other cases, it is a polite, non-confrontational and indirect way of refusing an offer or giving a reason why you did not choose a particular option.

Example:

Person A: Tam-mai teuh mâi pák têe bâan rao, yang ngai rao gâw mâi yòo – hâwng wâang yòo dee. Person B: Mâi bpen rai chún mâi kôi sà-dùak.

คนแรก: ทำไมเธอไม่พักที่บ้านเรา ยังไงเราก็ไม่อยู่ ห้องว่างอยู่ดี คนที่สอง: ไม่เป็นไร ฉันไม่ค่อยสะดวก

Person A: Why don't you stay at our place because we're not there (at that time) anyway – the place is free (available). Person B: That's ok, it's fine.

Notice the use of '*yang ngai*', which by itself means '*how*' but in the usage above means '*in any case*'; it is like saying *"in however way..."*. Make sense?

Person A: Bpai taan kâao gun mái? Person B: Kăw-tôht ná, wan née mâi sà-dùak bpai jing jing.

คนแรก: ไปทานข้าวกันไหม คนที่สอง: ขอโทษนะ วันนี้ไม่สะดวกไปจริงๆ

Person A: Want to go for dinner? Person B: Sorry, today is no good / I'm not available today.

Tips / in my experience / insight: *this is a very useful word in so many everyday situations where you get offered things where you might well feel the thing being offered is not convenient, or downright inconvenient, or not fit for purpose or whatever... but obviously it has to make sense...you can't use it for when your aircon is broken obviously! The point is it is a good way of being diplomatic or when you can't be bothered to explain all the drawbacks.*

Cultural insight / life in Thailand: Thai people are diverse

Yes, just like back home, believe it or not, Thai people are just as diverse. You will come across websites or Westerners who have lived in Thailand for a while who will tell you lots of stereotypes of what Thai people are like but you should take these with a pinch of salt...as with all stereotypes. Yes, there may be some common traits but it is equally easy to stereotype British, American, Japanese, French or almost any other people too.

*And more to the point, in terms of learning the language, try to mix with different parts of society to get a balanced perspective and hear a wider range of vocabulary and speaking styles. For example, it is simply not true that pronouns are **always** omitted – if you listen to Thai conversations across society, pronouns are sometimes very much a feature, as are other seemingly more formal expressions.*

77. dee jung leuy! ดีจังเลย

Meaning – great!

Context – you have come across the word 'dee' already, not least in the word for 'hello'. 'jung leuy' are just intensifiers.

Example:

Person A: (Kíd) Wâa jà jùd 'bpaa-dtêe' (party) wan gèuhd láeo gâw jà chuan pêuan pêuan tóok kon. Person B: Lĕuh? Dee jung leuy! Mâi dâi jeuh pêuan baang kon naan láeo.

คนแรก: (คิด) ว่าจะจัดปาร์ตี้วันเกิดแล้วก็จะชวนเพื่อนๆทุกคน คนที่สอง: เหรอ ดีจังเลย ไม่ได้เจอเพื่อนบางคนนานแล้ว

Person A: I think I am going to have a party for my birthday and invite all our friends. Person B: Really? Great! I haven't seen some of them for ages.

As I have said elsewhere in this book, it is worth repeating that if you are going to use English originating words that have been absorbed into Thai, you need to pronounce them in a Thai way. So, it is important to say 'bpaa-dtêe', not *'party'*, as you would in English. Yes, it might seem strange but it isn't really – there are lots of words brought into English from other languages and now pronounced as per English, not the original pronunciation.

78. châwp bàwk wâa ชอบบอกว่า

Meaning – likes to say / often says

Context – the use of 'châwp' is quite common in Thai and although it does mean '*likes to*' literally, the real meaning is usually to describe a characteristic of someone (because they '*like*' to do it). For example, if it was 'châwp kíd wâa', it might be more like '*always thinks*'.

Example:

Káo jà châwp bàwk wâa "bpáep neung", "dǐao maa", láeo gâw hǎi bpai...jon rao kíd wâa, mâi bpen rai, dǐao tam eng gâw dâai.

เขาจะชอบบอกว่า "แป๊ปนึง เดี๋ยวมา" แล้วก็หายไป จนเราคิดว่า ไม่เป็นไร เดี๋ยวทำเองก็ได้

He always says "I'm on the way", "One second" but never turns up, to the point where I am thinking, never mind, I'll do it myself.

Cultural insight / life in Thailand: Connect with Thais by fun

One of the best ways to connect with Thai people is through song. You must know already that one of the generalizations about Thai people is as close to being true as any generalization can be – the fact that Thais are fun loving people. And nothing is more fun than a night at karaoke Thai style.

Another way is to connect with another Thai trait – nationalism (in the best sense). Appreciate sports, especially the national sports teams and be aware of when the next big game is on and go along.

79. láw lên ล้อเล่น

Meaning – just kidding / teasing

Context – quite a useful word once you are good enough in Thai to make jokes and tease people (in a polite way).

Example:

Láw lên, láw lên, ná! Mâi dtâwng 'see-rêe-at' (serious).

ล้อเล่น ล้อเล่นนะ ไม่ต้องซีเรียส

Just joking ok, I didn't mean it.

Tips / in my experience / insight: *learn your '...lên' words and you will instantly have a very useful new set of words that will actually be relevant to your everyday conversation. You will be amazed how common these words are and how you ever missed them in your Thai friends' conversations before. For example:*

àan lên – *reading (casually or without concentrating)*

gin lên – *snacking*

pòod lên – *joking*

sài lên – *wearing something casually, maybe around the house*

doo lên – *watching (TV) but not particularly intently*

80. wái jai kôi mâi dâai ไว้ใจไม่ค่อยได้

Meaning – cannot trust

Context – the 'kôi', as you probably know already, softens the expression, just as 'really' does in the English translation.

Example:

Pôo-chaai nâa dtaa dee wái jai mâi dâai – práw múk jà jâo chóo!!

ผู้ชายหน้าตาดีไว้ใจไม่ได้เพราะมักจะเจ้าชู้

You can't trust any guy who's good looking – they're all players!

> **Tips / in my experience / insight:** you might be fooled into thinking every man is "*jâo chóo*" for Thai women because you will often hear this word levelled at Thai and Western men as well as some actors and so on. Many Thai pop songs are about men (and admittedly, less often, women) being unfaithful and the sadness that follows etc. I have heard people say all Thai songs are love songs but in my experience, most songs that people associate as being love songs are about some kind of love tragedy. As I mentioned right at the start, Thai songs are an excellent source for learning Thai – there used to be a site that had a massive database of song lyrics written out in the three languages along with an MP3 file of the song so you could listen and read simultaneously. If you find another such site, I highly recommend using it to learn Thai – not just informative but fun and culturally insightful.

81. bàep (wâa) แบบ

Meaning – it's like

Context – you know how some Americans use '*like*' as every other word in a sentence and sometimes even when they have finished, you still don't know what they meant? For example, "*you know, it's like…you know what I mean, I mean come on, and so he's like, and I'm like whaat, like…*". "Err…no, I don't think I do know what you mean…!" Well, guess what, Thai has its own version of this type of speech and it can be equally frustrating / amusing to listen to, depending on your point of view. You sometimes get sentences with multiple 'bàep's, 'gâw keu's and 'nôon, nêe, nân's and you have no idea what on earth the real point is!

Example:

Káo bpen bàep née dtâng naan laéo.

เขาเป็นแบบนี้ตั้งนานแล้ว

He has been like this for a long time.

> **Tips / in my experience / insight:** *although you may want to speak authentic Thai, using multiple 'bàep's and 'gâw keu's and basically implying a lot will not work for you like it does for native Thais…just as there are many ways of speech in English that are fine for native English speakers but if a foreigner speaking only basic English starts copying these, it either sounds out of place or comical or both!*

82. máe wâa jà แม้ว่าจะ

Meaning – no matter whether / what...

Context – as you saw earlier, 'tĕung máe' means 'even though' and 'máe' by itself means 'no matter'.

Example:

Máe wâa jà yáai bpai yòo bprà-têt èun gâw kong mâi dee tâo meuang tai ràwk.

แม้ว่าจะย้ายไปอยู่ประเทศอื่น ก็คงไม่ดีเท่าเมืองไทยหรอก

No matter what country you move to you probably won't find anywhere better than Thailand.

The use of 'kong' is quite common to this type of statement because it softens the strong opinion (even if the person actually fully believes in his opinion). Use 'kong' to impress local speakers with your cultural sensitivity.

> **Tips / in my experience / insight:** BTW, if you are to understand Thai culture and in short, the essence of being Thai, one of the key aspects is to understand the strong sense of national pride. And hopefully you will come to see this is one of the best things about Thailand – a great country with people who love their country. And even better, this topic is probably the best topic for you to practise your Thai – just start talking with a taxi driver about Thailand being great, the nice people etc and you are guaranteed to engage him and pick up lots of useful conversational language.

83. sùan yài ส่วนใหญ่

Meaning – mainly / normally / mostly

Context – we have already discussed 'sùan' before, which means '*part*' so 'sùan yài' is pretty logical i.e. '*on the part of the majority*' if you were to translate literally.

Example:

Sùan yài jà bpai àwk gam lang gaai dtawn săo aa-tít mâak gwàa.

ส่วนใหญ่จะไปออกกำลังกายตอนเสาร์อาทิตย์มากกว่า

Normally I prefer to go to the gym on weekends.

Chún mee pêuan yéuh. Sùan yài bpen pôo yĭng dtàe gâw mee pêuan pôo-chaai bâang.

ฉันมีเพื่อนเยอะ ส่วนใหญ่เป็นผู้หญิงแต่ก็มีเพื่อนผู้ชายบ้าง

I have lots of friends. Most of them are women but I have some male friends too.

84. rêuay rêuay เรื่อย ๆ

Meaning – on and on / going ok / continuously

Context – this is a commonly heard word in Thai and is quite difficult to use correctly for beginners, both in terms of pronunciation and also to get the context right.

Example:

Person A: <u>Bpen</u> <u>yang</u> <u>ngai</u> bâang? Person B: R<u>êuay</u> r<u>êuay</u>.

คนแรก: เป็นยังไงบ้าง คนที่สอง: เรื่อย ๆ

Person A: How are you doing? Person B: Ticking along nicely / Going ok / Living day to day (and many, many others).

Ráan née <u>bpen</u> têe <u>ní-yom</u> chûang née...lôok-káa <u>jà</u> <u>kâo</u> maa rêuay rêuay <u>táng</u> <u>wan</u>.

ร้านนี้เป็นที่นิยมช่วงนี้ ลูกค้าจะเข้ามาเรื่อย ๆ ทั้งวัน

This store / restaurant is really popular; customers are streaming in all day.

> **Tips / in my experience / insight:** *if you can get the pronunciation, which can be awkward for Westerners, this is a useful word and a good alternative to always saying "I'm fine" when people ask you "<u>Sa</u>-baai dee <u>mái</u>?" Another one of those words that gets you instant credit if you are at beginner level but trying to improve.*

85. ràwk หรอก

Meaning – no literal meaning

Context – this is one of the most important words to learn if you want to be able to converse in Thai and gain the respect of native speakers. It has no literal meaning and is simply a word to show humility or tone down an opinion or soften your rebuttal of someone else's comment. If you think about it, English speech uses the same concept (think: 'well, I'm not too sure about that...' as opposed to 'no, I don't agree!' and countless other examples) so it is not really a Thai thing, just a way of speaking that is more accommodating and polite.

Example:

Mun kong mâi châi yàng nán ràwk.

มันคงไม่ใช่อย่างนั้นหรอก

Well, I don't know if it's quite like that.

Mâi gèng ràwk, pôod dâai níd nòi eng.

ไม่เก่งหรอกพูดได้นิดหน่อยเอง

No, I'm not that good really, I can only speak a few words.

One of the things you will probably need to say most often as you get better at Thai and receive praise for your 'excellent' Thai.

Káo mâi tam yàng nán ràwk.

เขาไม่ทำอย่างนั้นหรอก

He won't / wouldn't do anything like that.

Dĭao maa ná, mâi naan ràwk.

เดี๋ยวมานะไม่นานหรอก

I'm coming ok, not long.

Person A: Lawng chim doo, a-ròi mâak. Person B: Mâi a-ròi ràwk – chún mâi châwp gin kǎwng pèt nà.

คนแรก: ลองชิมดู อร่อยมาก คนที่สอง: ไม่อร่อยหรอก ฉันไม่ชอบกินของเผ็ดน่ะ

Person A: Try it, it's really tasty. Person B: I don't like it – I don't really like spicy food to be honest.

> **Tips / in my experience / insight:** *use this word a lot! Listen for when Thai people use it and commit to memory. Often it will sound like "lawk", as many words in Thai and some other Asian languages have a relaxed pronunciation of 'r' to more like an 'l' sound in casual speech. If you are going to say it though, regardless of whether everyone around you says 'r' words with an 'l', you should always defer to correct pronunciation. Think about it – even if native English speakers mispronounce or colloquialise words, you would not teach a foreigner to speak like that, right?*

86. hèd-pǒn têe เหตุผลที่

Meaning – the reason that

Context – another pretty simple word to use so no further explanation needed.

Example:

Hèd-pǒn têe lêuak tam yàng nán gâw prâw wâa tâa mâi mee krai rêuhm tam gàwn gâw kong mâi dâi bpai nǎi.

เหตุผลที่เลือกทำอย่างนั้นก็เพราะว่าถ้าไม่มีใครเริ่มทำก่อนก็คงไม่ได้ไปไหน

The reason I chose to go ahead and do that is because if I don't take the first step we'll never get anywhere.

Teuh àad mee róoi hèd-pǒn têe teuh jà bpai dtàe chún mee piang hèd-pǒn diao jà hâi teuh yòo. Fung sǐang hǔa jai kǎwng chún láeo teuh àad-jà róo hèd-pǒn diao mee yòo gâw keu rúk teuh.

เธออาจมีร้อยเหตุผลที่เธอจะไป แต่ฉันมีเพียงเหตุผลเดียวจะให้เธออยู่ ฟังเสียงหัวใจของฉันแล้วเธออาจจะรู้ เหตุผลเดียวมีอยู่ก็คือรักเธอ

Maybe you've got 100 reasons to leave but I've only got one reason to make you stay. Listen to the sound of my heart and you will know that one reason is that I love you.

Some of you may know already that these are lyrics from a famous Thai song – 100 hèd-pǒn by Ster.

87. krai bàwk? ใครบอก

Meaning – who says?

Context – just as in English this can be a little blunt so use with care. Needless to say, always use 'krúp' / 'kà' with anyone apart from those who are very familiar or intimate to you, in order to make the word a little more polite.

Example:

Person A: Káo jà bpìd săa-kăa née laéo jà hâi pûak rao yáai bpai yòo săa-kăa dtrong Sà-yăam. Person B: Krai bàwk?

คนแรก: เขาจะปิดสาขานี้แล้วจะให้พวกเราย้ายไปอยู่สาขาตรงสยาม คนที่สอง: ใครบอก

Person A: They are going to close this branch and move us to the Siam branch instead. Person B: Who says?

Yâak lĕuh? Krai bàwk? Dĭao tam hâi doo.

ยากเหรอ ใครบอก เดี๋ยวทำให้ดู

It's difficult? Who says? I'll show you how it's done.

88. ná wan née ณ วันนี้

Meaning – as of today / now / as things stand

Context – the word 'ná' is the key here – it signifies something 'as of...'.

Example:

Ná wan née yang mâi mee krai sà-màk dtàe yang lĕua we-laa èeg săwng aa-tít.

ณ วันนี้ยังไม่มีใครสมัคร แต่ยังเหลือเวลาอีกสองอาทิตย์

Up until today nobody has applied but there's still two weeks to go.

Ná wan née gâw yang maa tam ngaan săai yòo. Maa tam ngaan săai săwng aa-tíd dtìd láeo. Tâa mâi bprùp bproong dtua dtâwng tòok lâi àwk nâe.

ณ วันนี้ ก็ยังมาทำงานสายอยู่ มาทำงานสายสองอาทิตย์ติดแล้ว ถ้าไม่ปรับปรุงตัวต้องถูกไล่ออกแน่

I'm still coming to work late – I've been late to work for two weeks in a row now. If I don't sort myself out, they're going to sack me for sure.

89. hâi (káo) tam ให้ทำ

Meaning – let him do / make him do / get him to do

Context – '<u>hâi</u>' is quite an interesting word in Thai. You probably know it as '*give*' and that is the simplest form of this word. The other uses of this word are still based on '*give*' but it takes a bit of understanding to see the link...it is something like "*give it to him to do*'.

Example:

Dǐao <u>jà</u> <u>hâi</u> <u>châng</u> maa <u>tam</u> <u>sǎo</u> aa-<u>tít</u>.

เดี๋ยวจะให้ช่างมาทำเสาร์อาทิตย์

I'll get the workman to come and fix it on the weekend.

> **Tips / in my experience / insight:** *this word can take some getting used to so listen out for it* – '<u>hâi</u>' *is used in many situations where you will get someone to do something like, for example, if your apartment or hotel has some issue, the management office or front desk would say that they will get a workman to come and take a look or whatever. Or you can also use it yourself if you want to refer to a person who you will get to help you.*

90. rěu mâi gâw หรือไม่ก็

Meaning – or if not then… / or otherwise…

Context – you can see how common 'gâw' is – it is omnipresent in everyday Thai speech. 'Rěu mâi' is pretty straightforward and just means '*or if not*'.

Example:

Tăeo née mee ráan sêua pâa yéuh yáe…rěu mâi gâw bpai Paragon gâw dâai tâa yàak jà séu pûak 'baen-nem' (brand name).

แถวนี้มีร้านเสื้อผ้าเยอะแยะ หรือไม่ก็ไปพารากอนก็ได้ถ้าอยากจะซื้อพวกแบรนด์เนม

There are loads of clothes shops around here…or you could go to Paragon if you want brand name stuff.

Wan née bpai tîao gan dee gwàa. Bpai doo năng mái rěu mâi gâw bpai séu DVD ao glàp maa doo têe bâan? Mee năng jàak bpee têe láeo têe yang mâi dâi doo têe yàak doo měuan gun. Teuh wâa ngai?

วันนี้ไปเที่ยวกันดีกว่า ไปดูหนังไหมหรือไม่ก็ไปซื้อดีวีดีเอากลับมาดูที่บ้าน มีหนังจากปีที่แล้วที่ยังไม่ได้ดูที่อยากดูเหมือนกัน เธอว่าไง

Let's go out today. Do you want to go to the cinema or if not, we could always buy a DVD and watch it at home. There's this film that I missed when it was out last year and I still want to see it. What do you think?

91. mâi róo dtua ไม่รู้ตัว

Meaning – not aware

Context – if you know the meaning of 'róo' and 'dtua' you know how this translates to not being aware. It literally means to not know yourself.

Example:

Pǒm châwp bòn mâak geuhn bpai jon baang kráng mâi róo dtua wâa gam lang bòn yòo.

ผมชอบบ่นมากเกินไปจนบางครั้งไม่รู้ตัวว่ากำลังบ่นอยู่

I tend to complain so much sometimes I am not even aware I am complaining!

Baang kráng kon rao gâw pôod a-rai àwk bpai dooy mâi róo dtua wâa sìng têe pôod gam-lang tam ráai jìt jai kon èun yòo.

บางครั้งคนเราก็พูดอะไรออกไปโดยไม่รู้ตัวว่าสิ่งที่พูดกำลังทำร้ายจิตใจคนอื่นอยู่

Sometimes people say things out loud without realizing that their words could hurt people's feelings.

92. sĭa daai / sĭa o-gàat

เสียดาย / เสียโอกาส

Meaning – missed a chance / what a shame

Context – another very common word in Thai and again, one of those words that is not spoken in exactly the same way as in English and therefore, rather interesting to learn. 'Sĭa o-gàat' is fairly simple and translates directly as you stating the fact that you have missed a chance whereas 'sĭa daai' is used as a word to mourn that missed opportunity, so sometimes complementary.

Example:

Sĭa daai jung! Bpen o-gàat têe dee mâak leuy. Bpò-kà-dtì káo mâi kăai tòok kà-nàad née.

เสียดายจัง เป็นโอกาสที่ดีมากเลย ปกติเขาไม่ขายถูกขนาดนี้

Oh man, we missed out on the sale! It was much cheaper than the normal price.

Rêep rêep jawng dtŭa dee gwàa jà dâi mâi plâat o-gàat.

รีบๆ จองตั๋วดีกว่าจะได้ไม่พลาดโอกาส

Better to book tickets soon so that we don't miss out.

I used plâat o-gàat **instead of** sĭa o-gàat.

93. mâi (dâi) mee jè-dtà-naa / mâi (dâi) dtâng jai
ไม่มีเจตนา / ไม่ตั้งใจ

Meaning – had no intention / didn't mean to

Context – these are two ways to say *'intention'*, where the former is probably a bit more formal and less commonly heard compared to the latter. Another reason is the difference between saying that someone had no intention to do and he / she did not mean to do – just as with English, the context will drive which word you choose.

Example:

Têe mâe pôod yàng nán gâw práw wâa mâe wăng dee gùp lôok. Mâe mâi dâi dtâng jai jà wâa lôok ná. Kâeh yàak hâi lôok lêuak taang àwk têe dee hâi gùp dtua eng kâeh nán eng. Tóok yàang mâe pôod bpai dûai jè-dtà-naa dee ná.

ที่แม่พูดอย่างนั้นก็เพราะว่าแม่หวังดีกับลูก แม่ไม่ได้ตั้งใจจะว่าลูกนะ แค่อยากให้ลูกเลือกทางออกที่ดีให้กับตัวเองแค่นั้นเอง ทุกอย่างแม่พูดไปด้วยเจตนาดีนะ

(Your mum speaking...) What I said, I said because I always want the best for you (my kids). I didn't mean to nag, I just want you to make sure you make the right choices in life, that's all. Everything I say, I say with your best interests at heart, you know that, right kids?

94. ngáw ง้อ

Meaning – to win back the love of your loved one by apologizing / to woo

Context – although I have not included any verbs in my list of 100 words, I thought this should be one of the exceptions as it is a verb that doesn't have an exact equivalent in English. Some people may translate it as *'to make up'* but this is not exactly the same as 'ngáw' and there is another word for this in Thai anyway – 'keun dee'. If you have had a Thai girlfriend (or maybe even a close Thai friend who you may have hurt in some way), you are bound to have come across this word. It goes to the heart of relationships in Thailand and the concept of a man should 'ngáw' a woman is central to your success in maintaining romantic or perhaps even non-romantic relationships.

Example:

Dĭao súk púk káo gâw maa ngáw, práw mâi yàng nán gâw jà dtâwng hăa kâao gin eng.

เดี๋ยวสักพักเขาก็มาง้อ เพราะไม่อย่างนั้นก็จะต้องหาข้าวกินเอง

You wait, pretty soon he's going to come and say sorry and try and make up, otherwise he knows he's going to have to get his own dinner tonight!

Kon têe kăai kăwng gèng jà róo wí-tee ngáw lôok-káa...mâi yàng nán kăai mâi kôi dâai ràwk.

คนที่ขายของเก่งต้องรู้วิธีง้อลูกค้า ไม่อย่างนั้นขายไม่ค่อยได้หรอก

People who are good at selling know how to please (suck up to / charm / service) customers, otherwise they wouldn't be that good at sales.

Person A: Yàak jà róo wâa jà mee pôo-yĭng têe ngáw pôo-chaai bpen mái. Person B: Jà bâa lĕuh? Pôo-yĭng jà ngáw pôo-chaai tam-mai? Pôo-yĭng tòok dtà-làwt! Pôo-chaai jâo chóo...paw róo wâa dtua eng pìt gâw dtâwng maa ngáw sì!

คนแรก: อยากจะรู้ว่ามีผู้หญิงที่ง้อผู้ชายเป็นไหม
คนที่สอง: จะบ้าหรอผู้หญิงจะง้อผู้ชายทำไม ผู้หญิงถูกตลอด ผู้ชายเจ้าชู้ พอรู้ว่าตัวเองผิด ก็ต้องมาง้อสิ

Person A: I wonder whether there are women who can apologize and make up to men. Person B: Are you crazy? Why on earth would women apologize and make up to men – it's men who like to play around and when they realize they are wrong, of course they have to beg to come back to us!.

Admittedly, the sentence above sounds a little more weird in English than in Thai. In Thai, sentiments such as the above and variations on that theme are not uncommon.

95. gaan têe (rao jà...) การที่

Meaning – no literal meaning

Context – as you no doubt know 'gaan' transforms a verb into a noun e.g. 'gaan tam ngaan' transforms the verb *'to work'* into the noun *'work'*. Of itself the word 'gaan' does not have any real meaning. So this expression cannot really be translated properly until you know what verb you are applying the *'gaan têe jà'* to.

Example:

Gaan têe rao jà kâo jai krai súk kon mun dtâwng chái we-laa sèuk-săa rian róo sêung-gun-láe-gun.

การที่เราจะเข้าใจใครสักคนมันต้องใช้เวลาศึกษาเรียนรู้ซึ่งกันและกัน

It takes time to get to know each other and really learn about them and understand them.

Notice two rather tricky words to learn – 'sêung', as per earlier in the book and 'gun-láe-gun'. In this example they are used to mean *'about each other'*.

Gaan têe gin kâao dtrong we-laa chûai hâi mâi oô-an.

การที่กินข้าวตรงเวลาช่วยให้ไม่อ้วน

Eating meals at regular meal times helps keep weight down.

96. nai têe sòot ในที่สุด

Meaning – in the end

Context – this is pretty straightforward so not much explanation required.

Example:

Nai têe sòot pǒm gâw chá-ná měuan deuhm.

ในที่สุดผมก็ชนะเหมือนเดิม

In the end I always win.

Koi doo sì, nai têe sòot tóok yàang gâw jà dtâwng jòp long dûai dee.

คอยดูสิ ในที่สุดทุกอย่างก็จะต้องจบลงด้วยดี

In the end everything will work out fine, you wait and see.

97. châng mun tèuh ช่างมันเถอะ

Meaning – forget it / don't worry about it / leave it

Context – a rather common expression among women, this is a word to show frustration or to move on when enough is enough. Men can still use this word.

Example:

Person A: <u>Tam</u>-mai káo mâi toh maa hăa <u>chún</u> leuy? Person B: <u>Mâi</u> <u>bpen</u> <u>rai</u> <u>ná</u> gae, châng mun tèuh. Hăa <u>mài</u> dee gwàa.

คนแรก: ทำไมเขาไม่โทรมาหาฉันเลย คนที่สอง: ไม่เป็นไรนะแก ช่างมันเถอะ หาใหม่ดีกว่า

Person A: Why doesn't he call me? Person B: Never mind, forget him. Let's go out and find someone else.

Notice the use of 'dee gwàa' which, in this case, is not translated. If we were to translate it, it would be like saying *"looking for a new boyfriend is better...(than not looking for one)"*.

'gae' is another pronoun that I will discuss in the next book. As a preview, trust me, you can't use it as a foreigner – it would sound weird.

98. práwm gùp พร้อมกับ

Meaning – along with

Context – 'práwm' means '*ready*' and so 'práwm gùp' means '*ready with*'.

Example:

Bâan lăng née kăi yòo têe săam láan dtòk dtàeng rîap róoi práwm 'fer-ni-jêuh' (furniture).

บ้านหลังนี้ขายอยู่ที่สามล้านตกแต่งเรียบร้อยพร้อมเฟอร์นิเจอร์

The house is going for B3m and comes with furniture.

Chún mâi yàak mee faen leuy jà bàwk hâi ná. Pôo-chaai nâ maa práwm gùp kwaam bpùat hŭa – kăw yòo kon dĭao dee gwàa, sa-baai jai gwàa yéuh.

ฉันไม่อยากมีแฟนเลย จะบอกให้นะ ผู้ชายน่ะมาพร้อมกับความปวดหัว ขออยู่คนเดียวดีกว่าสบายใจกว่าเยอะ

I don't want a boyfriend for sure. As far I'm concerned, I'm better off without a boyfriend – less hassle, less issues. I'm very happy with my simple single life just the way it is thank you.

Notice that I have not translated the sentence directly.

Also notice the 'kăw yòo' – in this scenario, the speaker isn't actually begging or even directing the statement at someone in particular. It is something like saying "*just let me be...*" i.e. you are requesting society. Learn this form of expression – it is common.

99. dĭao เดี๋ยว

Meaning – wait / you wait and see / no literal meaning

Context – literally, 'dĭao' does mean to wait but it is also used, as you will have seen in several of the example sentences already, to provide an implicit sense of waiting or just a rhythmic pause to the sentence. Confused? This is another of those words that you need to learn through developing a feel for the Thai.

Example:

Person A: Bpai wâai náam gun mái? Person B: Dĭao, èeg krêung chûa mohng.

คนแรก: ไปว่ายน้ำกันไหม คนที่สอง: เดี๋ยว อีกครึ่งชั่วโมง

Person A: Want to go swimming? Person B: Sure, give me half an hour.

Tâa bpai săwn dèk têe bâan káo, dĭao, mee bpan-hăa nâe leuy. Pâw mâe châwp maa kui dûai, tăam kam-tăam láeo gâw hâi kam náe-nam tóok kráng leuy.

ถ้าไปสอนเด็กที่บ้านเขาเดี๋ยวต้องมีปัญหาแน่เลย พ่อแม่ชอบมาคุยด้วย ถามคำถาม แล้วก็ให้คำแนะนำทุกครั้งเลย

Whenever I tutor kids at their home, there's always problems. Their parents always come and start chatting, asking questions and giving advice every single time.

The real meaning is parents 'sticking their nose in' but said in a Thai, toned down way.

Also notice that 'dïao' isn't translated into 'wait' explicitly but you can see where it fits in – in this case, it's basically the comma after 'home'.

Cultural insight / life in Thailand: Bargaining and haggling

So you go to Thailand and you cannot believe all the amazingly attractive goods at low prices and you have read guide books on the need to negotiate a good deal so you begin haggling to bring the price down even further. So you really get into it, start at a ridiculously low price and then when you get an indifferent or angry reaction from the seller or they mutter something about you under their breath and their legendary Thai smile disappears, you start to wonder what happened to the amazing customer service and wonderful people you were told of.

The simple lesson here is that you should know when to bargain (at a roadside clothes market) and when not (e.g. in a department store)to and how to ask for a discount (ask politely and always with the intention of BOTH of you getting a good deal).

Also, understand that some tourist area markets such as on Sukhumvit Road, where, yes, you as a foreigner will be targeted with higher quotes, are quite different to markets in Siam Square or Lardprao, for example, where prices are not so jacked up and the vendors are not getting a massive profit margin per item.

Most important, whether you are negotiating with a stallholder on Sukhumvit, or Siam, or in Chatuchak, or with a tradesman for some work at your condo, don't negotiate from the standpoint that you are being ripped off and forget your manners. And even more important, learn when it is right to stop haggling and just pay it – often you are haggling over a tiny amount in your own currency and the chances are the seller is not getting rich off you!

100. mùn sâi! หมั่นไส้

Meaning – the feeling when you say "*give me a break*" / can't stand that!

Context – you have probably heard this word, possibly even directed at you yourself and if you heard it and remember the context, you know what this word means. If you have not come across this word, it is very difficult to explain as there is no real equivalent in English. Basically it is a passive aggressive but also humorous word that is directed by a woman at either a man or a woman who is a bit full of himself / smug or in the case of woman vs. woman, it is a mild form of what Westerners would call bitchiness i.e. "look at her and her Prada handbag, waltzing around here like she owns the place". Or, think of it as a softer version of what Americans call "haters".

Men do not 'mùn sâi' other men or women! To 'mùn sâi' someone is the verb version and 'nâa mùn sâi' is someone who is or is doing something that is worthy of being 'mùn sâi'd. Get it? You will, once you go out and start showing off about something or look 'too happy' when everyone else around you is neutral or in a bad mood. Don't try and use it yourself if you are a man unless you do it deliberately to get a laugh or at least, less dramatically.

Example:

Dâai kâeh raang-wan têe săam gâw 'choh' (show) bpai tûa. Mùn sâi (jung)!

ได้แค่รางวัลที่สามก็โชว์ไปทั่ว หมั่นไส้ (จัง)

(Look at him...only) got third place and look at how much he's showing off. Totally over the top!

Did you notice the expression "'choh' bpai tûa"? I'll leave you to work it out.

Pôo-chaai kon née chái we-laa tam pǒm nâa grà-jòk naan mâak. Mùn sâi!

ผู้ชายคนนี้ใช้เวลาทำผมหน้ากระจกนานมาก หมั่นไส้

Omg, this guy spends ages in front of the mirror doing his hair! What a poser!

Dǐao faen teuh jà maa rúp bpai tîao condo káo lěuh…măe mùn sâi.

เดี๋ยวแฟนเธอจะมารับไปเที่ยวคอนโดเขาเหรอ แหม หมั่นไส้

Oh, your boyfriend is coming to pick you up and take you to his condo…well, it's alright for some!

Notice that the tone in the three sentences is slightly different – the last one is a softer sentiment by friends of the girl, not 'haters'. And BTW, notice that I have not translated directly e.g. the second Thai sentence doesn't say *'poser'* anywhere. And the first sentence could easily be ended as *"What a total…!"*.

> **Tips / in my experience / insight:** *I get 'mùn sâi'd quite often! It's probably because sometimes I seem like I am showing off or have a smug expression on my face when I have been proved right. If you're that kind of personality, be prepared to get 'mùn sâi'd.*

FURTHER LEARNING

So, I hope you have found this book useful. If you want to follow my method of learning Thai, you will need a practise partner who can help you bring the words in this book to life and help you test yourself on what you have learnt. With this in mind, I can wholeheartedly recommend the editor of this book, Kru Yuki. She is just as keen for you to speak Thai correctly and she shares the same principles on sounding Thai and speaking natural Thai that I do. Here is some further information on Kru Yuki:

Kru Yuki Tachaya is a professional native Thai teacher who has many years of experiences teaching Thai to foreigners. Her style of teaching focuses on natural-sounding practical Thai and skill practices. She offers private classes both via Skype and in person. Apart from that, she also offers 3 types of affordable self-study guiding services: "Write Like A Thai," "Speak Like A Thai" and "Ask Us Any Time." With these services, you can practice your Thai speaking and writing skills and have her check and correct the grammar, spelling and/or pronunciation for you. Since her focus has always been teaching foreigners to speak the way Thai people do, she's also going to help make your sentences sound more natural like the way native speakers would express themselves. With "Ask Us Any Time," you can send her questions about the Thai language that textbooks or dictionaries can't answer and she'll be able to help you. In addition to these services to help learners improve their Thai skills, she also offers language services: "Translation/interpretation," "Transcription" and "Voice Recording" for those of you who look for help with communication with Thai people. You can find more information about her private lessons and these helpful services at her official website: www.pickup-thai.com. The website also provides various free and fun lessons such as "Youtube Video Lessons," "Words Textbooks Don't Teach," "Real-Life Thai Conversations," "How Do You Say This in Thai?" and more! You can go there and practice your listening skills or learn something new about the Thai language, bit by bit every day.

Last but not least, kru Yuki Tachaya and her partner, kru Miki Chidchaya are the producers of the audio lesson series "PickupThai Podcast" - a unique innovative way of learning how to speak Thai naturally. PickupThai Podcast teaches 100% authentic Thai, rather than dry and unnatural textbook Thai that most teaching materials do. You will get to learn a variety of cool colloquial expressions that are commonly used by native speakers but never mentioned in textbooks written for foreigners. Every lesson is based on a fun story and filled with humor. It's educational and entertaining at the same time. If you have never been thrilled about learning Thai, you are going to experience fun for the first time with their quality materials. As each lesson only costs $5.89 and they have all-year-long value packages, plus frequent seasonal promotions, this could also be another alternative of learning Thai with a low budget. Below are example sentences taught in PickupThai Podcast.

แม่เลี้ยงซินเดอเรลล่าเนี่ยเหรอใจร้าย ฉันว่าใจดีต่างหาก ปล่อยให้อยู่กับผู้ชายถึงเที่ยงคืน

Cinderella's stepmother is mean? I think she's kind! She let her stay with a guy until midnight!

มีซะที่ไหน คนที่ขนาดกล้องค้างแล้วยังดูหล่อ

There are no guys who still look good even when their webcams freeze!

ไม่ได้จะแย่งกินสักหน่อย แค่ลองฝึกใช้ตะเกียบ

I wasn't going to steal your food from you. I was just practicing how to use chopsticks

เราก็รู้ว่าเขาไม่ชอบอากาศหนาว แต่ก็ไม่นึกเลยว่าบ้านเขาที่กรุงเทพจะติดฮีตเตอร์ด้วย

I knew he didn't like cold weather but I did not imagine that his house in Bangkok would have a heater.

ไหนๆก็ฟังเมียบ่นมาตั้งสี่ชั่วโมงแล้ว ฟังแม่บ่นต่ออีกหนึ่งชั่วโมงจะเป็นอะไรไป

You listened to your wife preach for four hours. It won't hurt if you listen to your mom preach for another hour.

Find more information about PickupThai Podcast and follow her on Facebook or Twitter to get updates on the free lessons posted on PickupThai from these links below:

Official Website: http://www.pickup-thai.com
Youtube Channel: http://www.youtube.com/user/pickupthai
Facebook Page: https://www.facebook.com/pickupthai
Twitter: https://twitter.com/pickupthai
Email: yuki.tachaya@pickup-thai.com

www.ingramcontent.com/pod-product-compliance
Lightning Source LLC
Chambersburg PA
CBHW021106080526
44587CB00010B/409